WHATEVER HAPPENED TO THE DINOSAURS?

You have never seen a live dinosaur—and neither has anyone else. But you do have an idea of what dinosaurs looked like and how they lived. They were incredible animals living in an incredible world. It was an environment very unlike the earth we know today. But, then, the dinosaurs disappeared. Why? How? Scientists had been trying to find an answer to this for a long time. Suddenly, new facts and theories started to attract attention, and many scientists began to look at dinosaurs differently. Did the dinosaurs completely vanish from the face of the earth—or are they still around today in a different form? Read on and you will discover many unusual things about these animals, in a fantastic journey through time and the animal kingdom.

WHATEVER HAPPENED TO THE
DINOSAURS?

William Jaber

Drawings by the Author

JULIAN MESSNER
New York

Manufactured in the United States of America

Design by Irving Perkins

Library of Congress Cataloging in Publication Data

Jaber, William.
    Whatever happened to the dinosaurs?

    Bibliography: p. 154
    Includes index.
    SUMMARY: Explores theories concerning the evolution
and extinction of dinosaurs and the environmental conditions in which they lived.
    1. Dinosauria—Juvenile literature.   [1. Dinosaurs.
2. Paleontology]   I. Title.
QE862.D5J24   568′.19   78–15939
ISBN 0–671–32872–7

To Dorothy Ferraro Jaber
Many times her love has turned my despair
into our victory.

Acknowledgments

The material for this book came from a wide variety of sources, including field study and direct observation of fossils. The most valuable single source, however, has been the written works of notable living paleontologists, biologists, and geologists. These are D. I. Axelrod, Robert T. Bakker, Albert F. Bennett, Edwin C. Colbert, Richard Cowen, Bonnie B. Dalzell, W. R. Dawson, Adrian J. Desmond, Peter Dodson, Carl O. Dunbar, Alan Feduccia, Robert A. Long, John H. Ostrom, Ronald P. Ratkevich, Armand Ricqlès, Alfred S. Romer, L. S. Russell, George G. Simpson, William E. Swinton, and Theodore Wexler.

Since many of these scientists represent opposing points of view, I have tried to present their positions with care and accuracy. I take full responsibility for any failure, fault, or error. The principal conclusions reached in this book are the author's own and must not be interpreted to represent any opinion or view other than that of the author himself.

I also had the benefit of the advice and counsel of Dr. Eugene Gaffney, curator of vertebrate paleontology at the American Museum of Natural History in New York City. I thank Dr. Gaffney for his valuable assistance.

I thank also my editor, Iris Rosoff, for her encouragement and criticism; my wife, Dorothy, for expending her valuable time in typing the manuscript; and Jean Joseph Robinson for reading and recommending a number of changes that were made in the manuscript.

CONTENTS

INTRODUCTION

No human being has ever seen a live dinosaur. Some very reputable scholars dispute this statement; yet, no one has ever been able to document such a sighting. Most scientists scoff at literature that seeks to prove the existence of dinosaurs. A book such as *On the Track of Unknown Animals* by B. Heuvelmans presents no clear photos or specimens (dead or alive). Nothing short of these is acceptable, because such evidence is a minimal requirement which zoologists, ornithologists, and botanists place upon themselves in their quests for new species.

As we shall see, the scientific conception of dinosaurs has always been vulnerable and subject to change. But scientists do not regard this vulnerability as a way of being free to establish irrational or unscientific reconstructions and ill-conceived images of what dinosaurs looked like in real life. Such activities violate our obligation to convey truth to our children during their impressionable school years.

One purpose in writing this book is to put before the reader a soundly researched, rationally derived conception of the dinosaurs, together with some notion of what the dinosaurs' world looked like. The only proper way to accomplish this is to listen to what scientists have to say about these prehistoric animals and then express the acquired information in comprehensible words and in picture reconstructions that carry scientific conclusions. Only in this manner can we avoid misinforming students or nonspecialists.

There are two widespread, erroneous conceptions regarding dinosaurs: one invented by the motion picture industry, with considerable help from science-fiction and television writers; the other a children's version which is the overly simplified, combined product of comic strip artists and children's book writers.

The motion-picture dinosaurs were usually poorly researched, imaginary creatures, fabricated to incorporate an unyielding ferocious savagery. Their physiology and anatomy were reconstructed solely for drama and entertainment and had little to do with education or science. The objective was to provide a vehicle in which to advance vicarious violence. The animals are destroyed as scientific objects but preserved as monsters in the popular imagination.

The children's dinosaurs usually deviate in the opposite direction—on the side of peaceful anthropomorphism; that is, the dinosaurs are given human traits such as childlike innocence, or they are conceived as lazy, docile animals that can be climbed upon and ridden like a horse. In one version, the dinosaur is a fairly accurate representation of an animal the paleontologists have named *Diplodocus.* In real life this animal had a long neck and very long tail. It stood on four huge postlike legs and was a grazing plant eater that lived along coasts or in swamps and marshes. A very fine skeleton of Diplodocus can be seen in the Carnegie Museum at Pittsburgh.

The children's Diplodocus, such as the famous comic strip dinosaur "Diny" of some years ago, had a long neck topped with a smiling snake's head. In this and some other versions, the dinosaur is given plates along its back so as to look like a Chinese dragon. One of these popular dinosaurs is facetiously dubbed "Puff the Magic Dragon" by some paleontologists in honor of the song of that title.

One of the media's arguments in favor of circulating ill-conceived representations of dinosaurs is that such impressions are better than none at all. But the scientist and teacher agree that a distortion of truth is very often, if not always, worse than no information at all.

Most of this book is directly concerned with the presentation of what is factually known about dinosaurs. But a strong attempt is made to deal with misconceptions that have come about mainly because of the motion picture industry.

Scientists, teachers, and students are confronted with three difficulties: they have to contend with possible outdating in their books and ideas (because of changing scientific data and new discoveries); they must keep up with the flood of new information and revisions in old information; and finally, they must help to undo erroneous conceptions that were perpetuated by some careless but influential media.

The old cliché that "truth is stranger than fiction" is especially appropriate to the subject of dinosaurs. There is no need to distort or mislead the reader. All that is necessary is to put in a little extra effort to learn what paleontologists already know: dinosaurs were incredible animals, living in an incredible world. Descriptions of their world sound like discussions concerning another planet.

Piles of poorly preserved skeletal remains and some tracks in stone are nearly all the evidence we have that dinosaurs ever existed. People have known about this evidence for less than 200 years. In fact, the name *dinosaur* was invented in Great Britain in 1841.

The present scientific conception of dinosaurs began with the work of Sir Richard Owen (1804–1892), the British physician-zoologist who invented the name dinosaur. In Owen's time there was one particular group of bones of prehistoric animals that had been regarded as the remains of large, lizardlike animals. But on the basis of their large size and other evidence, he could not agree that these had been lizards in real life. Many of his fellow scientists disagreed. They felt that several lizardlike qualities were present. In reality, there was little evidence for a definite decision either way.

But there was enough evidence in the remains to permit keeping the animals in the major class to which the modern lizards belong—the class of *reptiles*. Besides lizards, the class includes snakes, crocodiles, alligators, and turtles. Owen, therefore, agreed with most of his contemporaries that certain of the prehistoric animal remains were those of reptiles, but he refused to go so far as to call them lizards. Instead, he set up a special group of extinct reptiles—dinosaurs. Thus, the present conception of dinosaurs as a separate reptile group is based upon Owen's decision.

Owen had very little to work with in making his decision. No complete skeleton was then available. Moreover, no parts other than skeletal ones were preserved. There was no way to tell color, age, sex, or type of skin, such as whether any of the animals had hair, feathers, or scales. Also, the general shape, the mode of walking, and the habits of the animals remained a mystery. These could be guessed at, but the possibility of error was great. We should emphasize that because fossil evidence was sparse and unreliable, mistaken pronouncements about prehistoric animals were common in those days. Tools and technology were inadequate to achieve high accuracy in reconstructing dinosaurs.

At first, paleontologists felt comfortable with Owen's decision. All through the nineteenth century and up to about 1930, the study of dinosaurs expanded rapidly. Dinosaur exhibits in great museums attracted more visitors than any other exhibit.

Twentieth-century science began to fill in some of the data gaps. More became known about the dinosaurs: their mode of walking or running; how they stalked or killed their prey; what they ate; what their homeland might have been like in climate and geography; how the animals developed; and what assemblage of animals they were derived from. Other knowledge that Owen would have been astounded to know was learned about these animals.

By the mid-twentieth century, many scientists had begun to feel uneasy with Owen's decision to keep dinosaurs in the class of reptiles. For one thing, so many new kinds of dinosaurs were being discovered that a whole range of sizes and types had been added to the dinosaur group. Two major groups—a "bird-hip" group and "lizard-hip" group—began to be recognized among the new discoveries.

New data, acquired with the aid of more modern research techniques, began to cast suspicion on the name dinosaur itself. The name was rapidly losing its scientific value. Animals as different as cows are to horses were being called dinosaurs. Dinosaurs no bigger than chickens were classified in the same groups that the largest land animals that ever lived on this planet were. It was becoming obvious that the dinosaur had become more of a mystery than at any time since Owen invented the word in 1841.

About 1965, new information began pouring in at a rate which far exceeded the time available to paleontologists (those who study life of the distant past) for recording, analyzing, and absorbing the data. Periodically, they had to wade through reams of monographs, theses, published results of experiments, and reports from workers in the field who were discovering, excavating, and examining new fossil material.

In addition to this, paleontologists were finding that a great deal of what had been learned about dinosaurs in the past 200 years was now being questioned or was being subjected by their fellow workers to rigorous new tests for validity.

Consequently, a wave of uncertainty swept through the field of paleontology. Tempers flared as new theories arose and were aired in the media. Some leading paleontologists published scientific papers that questioned many current ideas about dinosaurs. These papers and the general dialogue which took place with each major new fossil discovery brought forth many changes. Some of the changes resulted from new data acquired as spin-off benefits from the space exploration programs.

Today, paleontology is in a state of ferment. Much of the frenzied studies and exciting debates center on a whole range of events and conditions which were discovered to have happened or to have existed in the distant past—events and conditions that had an effect on the evolution of dinosaurs.

Among these are the movement of whole continents, and the birth and death of great oceans. These events did not happen overnight. It took millions of years for such movements, but they had worldwide consequences.

The search to reveal the broad outlines of these movements is an international undertaking that has given rise to a new discipline—a field of knowledge known as *planetary geology*, or "global geology."

We shall review the achievements of global geology, which is a product of science in the 1970s. Our main purpose is to try and discover how much the movement of continents and the birth and death of oceans affected the evolution of the dinosaurs.

One bold new theory is that dinosaurs began their evolution from a large supercontinent under very warm, moist climates. After the supercontinent broke up, climates were altered, and environments were affected. The dinosaurs undoubtedly would have been affected by these events, too.

The idea that a supercontinent once existed is derived from the new science of *plate tectonics*. Plate tectonics assumes that very large-scale crustal movements of the earth have occurred in the distant past and are still occurring. Paleontologists, concerned with the development of dinosaurs, reasoned that, given enough time, such crustal movements, which involved whole continents, would have caused equally large-scale changes in climates and in the environments of living things. Paleontologists also note that plate tectonics explains the presence in the distant past of tropical vegetation (as seen in fossils) in the presently frigid Greenland. It also explains the presence of coal (made from plant matter) and the fossils of extinct life in Antarctica, where no plants or land animals except birds exist today.

So much new information has come to light that we can now reconstruct, although still in blurred outline, the dinosaurs' homelands and environments.

CHAPTER 1

Earliest Fossil Studies and the Founding of Historical Geology

Exploration and study that led to the discovery of dinosaurs began over 2,000 years ago in ancient Greece. Scholars there had long been collecting and examining fossils. They never understood clearly how fossils came to be found in the rocks, but the Greeks were the first to regard them as remains of living things. *Fossils* are mostly the hard parts of plants and animals, such as shells, bones, leaves, and branches, or they are a record of life such as footprints or impressions in stone. Fossils are preserved in the rocks by natural processes.

Herodotus (484–324 B.C.), the "father of history," and Aristotle (384–322 B.C.), the founder of the science of *natural history*, were the first to speculate on the origin and nature of fossils. They thought fossils were eggs or seeds which sprouted up in the rocks long after the animal or plant had been buried. Also, at that time, and right up to about 150 years ago, most people thought animals such as mice, flies, and other insects sprang full-grown from the rocks by a mysterious process known as *spontaneous generation*. These ideas were based on casual observations, not on carefully controlled experiments or scientific reasoning.

Nevertheless, the Greeks and, later, the Romans, were more advanced in their thinking about fossils than were most of the scholars of western Europe during the next 1,000 years following the decline of the Greco-Roman civilization.

Early Christians discouraged free investigations and the questioning of nature. Students and teachers alike were forbidden by Church rules and by threats of punishment (either by Church law or by God himself) to doubt the accuracy and validity of the Scriptures.

Once freedom of learning was stifled, Greco-Roman science faded, and it fled from Europe, taking refuge in Arabic or Moslem centers of learning in the Middle East. Arab scholars pursued natural history, Greek science and philosophy, and Roman law and engineering. They improved on them all and sheltered them for the next 1,000 years.

RENAISSANCE.   Spurred on by a series of religious Crusades against Islam (A.D. 1095–1204), Europeans invaded Arabic and Moslem lands. Although they were at war, they came into contact at several points with a polished, sophisticated Moslem-Jewish scholarship. Manuscripts and learning began to filter slowly back across the Mediterranean Sea into western Europe. After the Crusades, Europeans gradually borrowed back the Greco-Roman learning.

The Crusades stirred a new spirit of speculation—a rebirth of learning—known as the *Renaissance*. It began in Italy in about 1300. This new spirit of inquiry triggered fierce opposition from the clergy. The Church's response generated a great revival in religious fervor.

The notorious Inquisition for the punishment of heresy was begun in 1233 by Pope Gregory IX and continued in force throughout most of the Renaissance period. Thousands of students and teachers were tried and tortured, and many were murdered, rather than recant their beliefs. There were genocidal attacks and much other violence, sparked by the Church authorities in their war against secular learning; that is, learning pursued outside the Church and unsupervised by the Church.

Religious opposition remained effective and dangerous until well into the eighteenth century, when science began an explosive expansion, particularly in Great Britain and northern Europe.

THE NATURE OF RELIGIOUS OBJECTIONS.   The main barrier to the study of fossils was the Christian belief in *Special Creation.* This doctrine maintains that God created the earth in six days. It includes an assumption that all living things that were present at Creation are still present. God did not experiment with animals and plants—God is perfect and does not need to do so. Thus, there could be no extinct living things, nor any new ones, either. This refutes modern ideas on evolution. Finally, the doctrine regards the earth as being less than 6,000 years old—far too young to account for the formation of fossils and the physical features of the earth's surface (mountains, rivers, canyons, and so on). The intellectual climate surrounding this creationist doctrine ran strongly against science.

Among the powerful and influential pronouncements which had as their purpose to impose religious views of Creation on students of natural history was one by Archbishop Ussher, an Irish prelate. In 1564, Ussher proclaimed that he had discovered the exact date of Creation: it was 9:00 A.M., October 26, 4004 B.C.

A few years later, another authority issued an equally astounding statement: Noah's Great Deluge happened on November 18, 2349 B.C. Unfortunately for science, millions of people believed both dates, and they were thereafter entered as margin notations in most printed Bibles. Even today, millions of people who have never heard of Archbishop Ussher still believe that these dates are revealed Scripture. For the next 200 years, students of natural history either believed these dates and accepted them, or they labored in opposition to those who did.

Despite clerical opposition, however, fossil hunting was revived and became a part-time activity of many learned men. (Because of their subservient condition, there were very few women involved in Renaissance science.)

RELIGION AND SCIENCE TODAY. Today liberalism in ideas and freedom of thought permit the holding of beliefs and ideas that are seemingly in opposition to the doctrines of various religions. The main reason for this is that we now recognize two kinds of knowledge: one that is regarded as *revealed truth,* and which must be followed on faith alone, and the other is *science*, which does not require an act of faith to be valid. Facts that are the products of science are not revealed truth in any sense. They are not even sacred. They are simply summaries of observations or the results of both deductive and inductive reasoning, perhaps arrived at through experimentation over long periods of time. Scientific facts are disproven every day.

The lack of permanency of facts in science is the main reason for all the excitement in the field of paleontology today—a number of facts about dinosaurs, formerly accepted *almost* as acts of faith, have suddenly come under fire.

The age of the earth, its manner of creation, and the living things on the earth can all be studied in two ways: by resorting to faith and revealed truth, or by resorting to science. *Neither has anything to do with the other.* Science does not and cannot deny Biblical facts because such facts are accepted as articles of faith, and not as science. Civilized people in our modern world do permit this freedom to each other—examples of such toleration and conviviality can be seen in any classroom in any college in our nation, and in most countries of the world.

Scientific facts must always be open to question because *they are not articles of faith.* Even the fact that the sun will rise tomorrow has to be questioned, since there is no guarantee in science that it will rise tomorrow.

Although natural science and the study of fossils between 1500 and 1700 shared the fate of astronomy, medicine, and other sciences in being set back by the fury of Church opposition to their secular aspects, there was already enough momentum in progress to insure steady growth. Breaking down the wall of religious dogmatism occurred slowly. It was largely completed by 1700.

The freedom of scientific thought was obtained at a tragic cost, however. Among the great scholars lost was Giordano Bruno (1548–1600), who was burned at the stake. Others were caught in threatening situations, chiefly in denunciation and trial by the Inquisition. Most of them got away with their lives if they recanted their science. One who did recant, but still left us a legacy of great science, was Galileo Galilei (1564–1642). He was convicted of heresy and forced to recant.

Fossil collecting became more popular after 1500. Most collectors managed to stay clear of trouble with the authorities because their science—natural history—was still in a primitive stage of growth. Most fossil collectors of that time held acceptable beliefs regarding the nature of fossils and their origin. The principal theory used to explain the origin of fossils was that they were really *pseudomorphs*—forms and shapes that God tried out and rejected. He left the rejects in the rocks as fossils. Curiously enough, this belief did question the perfection of God (a perfect God would not need to experiment with different shapes and forms of animals and plants), yet it was acceptable to most Church authorities.

The most common belief—and one that was in complete

agreement with Christian theology of the time—was that fossils were the remains of living things that died during the Great Deluge. They were the animals that Noah could not or did not take aboard the ark. They were not on his passenger list, so to speak. People who held this belief were called *creationists*. Many famous scientists, and at least one of the founders of dinosaur studies, were creationists. We shall meet this scientist in Chapter 3.

There was one Renaissance scientist who denied special creation and other scriptural facts but did not suffer punishment for doing so. He escaped unharmed because he wrote most of his science in secret notebooks which were published long after his death.

He is Leonardo da Vinci (1452–1519), unquestionably the greatest scientist of the Renaissance. The period of modern fossil studies begins with Leonardo. By this time, no one person could possibly learn all there was to know about the science of natural history. Leonardo was probably the last ever to try, however.

During his lifetime, the sciences began to divide up into separate fields of study, or branches. Soon, all the modern sciences existed in general outline—biology, geology, chemistry, and physics, among others.

As we consider Leonardo's conclusions, it will become clear that science had entered upon its main course of development. Let us now see how the study of dinosaurs benefited from the work of Leonardo.

LEONARDO AND THE FOUNDERS OF HISTORICAL GEOLOGY.   Dinosaurs are known only from fossils. But no one could have learned about dinosaurs until fossils came to be regarded as evidence of past life. Leonardo da Vinci was the first to dispute the Great Deluge origin of some fossils. For a time, his interest centered on seashells that he found in the rocks of northern Italy, 250 miles from the nearest sea (the Adriatic Sea). In real life the shells had belonged to clams. Leonardo asserted that they could not have traveled to this site from the sea in forty days—the duration of the Great Deluge.

In addition to this argument, Leonardo also noted that the condition and nature of the fossils made it almost certain that they were not deposited in one great flood, but had been dropped or had traveled to the spot of burial over very long periods, and at several different times. In other words, the clams, if they were brought to the site of discovery, were brought by a series of small events, not by one large flood.

Finally, Leonardo clinched his argument that these shells had nothing to do with Noah's flood when he noted that the seashells in question were found in the rocks in association with other forms of marine (that is, oceanic) life. This clearly suggested to Leonardo that they were not even brought there. They *lived* there, *died* there, and became *buried* in the same spot.

The only possible conclusion to be made from this was that the particular spot was once the bottom of an ancient sea. It had by some unknown means been elevated to far above the present sea level. It was Leonardo's idea that finally won out over all other theories and beliefs, but it took 200 years and the help of many great scholars who came later.

THE FOUNDING OF HISTORICAL GEOLOGY. Among the first to pick up and expand on the ideas of Leonardo da Vinci was Nicolaus Steno (born Neils Stenson), 1638–1686, a Danish churchman. He was the first to recognize that rocks in a top layer were certain to be younger than the rocks underneath in the same layer. This was the principle of *superposition,* which is still a basic principle of geology. For his work with rock layers, Steno is regarded as one of the founders of *historical geology,* the science of the earth's history in the distant past.

A group of English scholars continued from where Steno left off and completed the basic framework of historical geology. Robert Hooke (1635–1703), a brilliant mechanical engineer, suggested that fossils were the remains of long-extinct life and that they could be used for determining the age of rock layers (strata).

John Ray (1628–1705) was a naturalist who described over 18,000 different plants. He was also among the first modern scholars to declare that fossils were the remains of extinct animals and plants.

William Smith (1769–1839) actually used fossils for age determination. He identified fossils that were peculiar to each layer. Therefore, whenever he saw the same fossils, he was certain that the rocks were of the same age as rocks elsewhere which contained those same fossils.

James Hutton (1726–1797) is often regarded as the father of historical geology. He was the first to argue openly that the earth was very ancient and that geological features such as mountains and coasts were changed in the past by the same forces in operation today—running water, wind, volcanoes, earthquakes. His famous axiom, "The present is the key to the past," is still a basic principle in historical geology. Hutton formulated the doctrine of *uniformitarianism,* which means that any feature on the earth could be produced, changed, or destroyed by the forces presently operating to effect these results—that is, the forces noted above.

CHAPTER 2

The Founding of Paleontology and the Study of Dinosaurs

By 1800, there were two main streams of research dealing with fossils: studies by historical geologists such as Smith and Hutton, seeking to establish the age and origin of the earth's major features, and the studies conducted for the primary purpose of learning about the animals and plants that lived in the distant past. Those who followed the latter course became paleontologists.

At the same time, the larger science disciplines had begun to break up into smaller, more manageable branches of study. The most important new science to appear at that time was geology, which had split away from natural history. No sooner had this occurred then geology also began to split up into a number of branch subjects. Two of these subjects were the two directions of fossil research—the study of fossils to determine the age of the earth and its features, and the study of fossils to learn about the plants and animals of the past.

The latter course of study had begun to develop from the time of da Vinci, when interest in fossil collecting had begun to spread to persons in the life science professions—medicine, zoology, and botany, for example. *Paleontology* is the

27

name given to the branch of historical geology that arose from these fossil studies by life scientists.

Those who studied fossils for the purpose of determining the age of the earth founded the sciences of *geomorphology* (formerly known as physiography, in the United States), which is the study of land forms; *stratigraphy*, the study of rock formations; and several others, mostly divisions of geology.

Paleontology, the study of life in the past, is made up from the Greek words *paleo*, meaning "old," and *onto*, meaning "being," and *logos*, meaning "discourse." The full literal meaning is "discourse on ancient being." However, the Greeks would never have used the words in this manner.

To the two main streams of fossil studies we should perhaps add a third one: clerical scholarship, directed toward the refutation of any interpretation of fossils that did not agree with the Scriptures. Moreover, clerics hoped to prove by their course of studies that fossils represented the remains of animals killed in the Great Deluge. Naturally, this group of scholars did not always study fossils using the scientific methods, but more often studied them within the confines of revealed faith. There were some important exceptions, however.

Clerical scholars were usually found in opposition to the group of scientists who became the founders of paleontology. This situation lasted until about 1870, when Darwinian evolution gained the upper hand and retained the gross allegiance of scientists. Thereafter, organized clerical opposition faded and was replaced by the hit-and-run sporadic fervor of fundamentalists in religion. That opposition was not inconsequential, however, as is attested to in the twentieth century by such events as the Scopes trial of 1925, in Dayton, Tennessee.

Two of the most important life scientists of the early nineteenth century were the Frenchmen Baron Léopold Chrétien Cuvier (1769–1832), and Jean Baptiste Lamarck (1744–1829). Cuvier and Lamarck very often found themselves on opposite sides in the debates and discussions that came out of fossil studies. Each represented a broadly different spectrum of learning in their society. Cuvier was a devout Christian who believed in Special Creation as described in the book of Genesis of the Bible, while Lamarck was not confined to the Scriptures in his beliefs.

Cuvier and Lamarck often engaged in blistering intellectual disputes, some of which were derived from basic religious differences. Because of their stature, they became leaders of two major factions in science, based on their respective views.

Although Cuvier was a "creationist"—that is, he followed the biblical version of Creation—he was not in strict agreement with it. He believed there was not just one, but several Creations, each following a worldwide disaster, or *catastrophe*. This doctrine of *catastrophism* was in direct opposition to Lamarck's ideas on the origin of the earth and the development of life.

Cuvier's catastrophism also conflicted with the views of James Hutton regarding how the earth developed. (See Chapter 1.) Cuvier believed that each time God destroyed the earth he populated it anew. Some plants and animals had to be newly created to replace those made extinct in the catastrophes. *Extinction* means the complete disappearance of a whole group, such as an entire species (for example, all dogs or all cats), or of a genus containing several species, such as all cattle.

Cuvier studied fossils so carefully that he was regarded as the world's leading authority on prehistoric life. Because his opinion was so greatly respected, other fossil hunters often brought their discoveries to him for identification and classification. It was in this manner that Cuvier was able to study and classify many of the animals which later became known as dinosaurs. (Cuvier died nine years before that term was invented by Sir Richard Owen.)

It was Cuvier who studied and classified the famous Meuse Lizard, now called *Mosasaurus*, a lizardlike prehistoric reptile whose discovery led directly to the study of dinosaurs. Cuvier's belief that this animal was a reptile prompted other paleontologists to classify many similar fossils as reptiles, too. This started an argument that has continued down to the present time. It is the question of whether dinosaurs are reptiles. As we shall see, that argument may be about to be resolved in the late 1970s.

The classification of the mosasaur was not the only classification by Cuvier that generated arguments, however, despite his great reputation. Many of his contemporaries viewed with alarm his identification of one particular fossil as the tooth of a rhinoceros. As it turned out, he was wrong—the tooth was that of an *Iguanodon,* a type of dinosaur, and the first dinosaur to be discovered. Actually, Cuvier was often wrong, but he was not ashamed of admitting to error. He handled so many fossils during his career that his percentage of error was quite small, considering the poor tools and methods in use at the time. His perceptive mind made efficient use of the limited information available. Unquestionably, Baron Cuvier is a major founder of dinosaur studies and of paleontology.

Jean Lamarck had little to do directly with the study of dinosaurs, but his indirect influence was enormous, probably greater even than that of Cuvier. The reason for this is that Lamarck had a more modern conception of prehistoric life and of the earth's origin. He is known in science as an "evolutionist." This means that Lamarck regarded life as being very ancient and having developed slowly through millions of years.

Lamarck was an expert classifier of plants and animals. He is regarded as the founder of the science of invertebrate paleontology—the study of animals without backbones that lived in the past (ancient mollusks, clams, worms, crustaceans, and others).

Lamarck made errors, too. And they were probably more serious than those of Cuvier; Lamarck so brilliantly expressed his facts that many scientists did not bother to analyze his work carefully. As a result, some of Lamarck's errors were accepted as truth right on through to the mid-twentieth century.

In their day, paleontology was hampered by the lack of reliable tools, inadequate methods of research, and a meager supply of fossils on which to base conclusions. Given these conditions, little could be learned directly from the fossils. Consequently, speculations, guesses, and indirect inferences formed a high percentage of what was then known about fossils.

For example, Lamarck argued that an organism acquired traits as a result of needs it met within its environment. The traits that satisfied these needs were often passed on to the next generation by inheritance. The twentieth-century science of heredity proved him wrong.

Lamarck was, however, the chief defender of the concept of evolution against the catastrophists and creationists, represented best by Cuvier. Lamarck's work prepared the intellectual climate for the introduction of the momentous Darwinian theory on evolution. This introduction took place thirty years after Lamarck's death, when Darwin published the first of two epic works on evolution. Darwin never admitted his indebtedness to Lamarck and even considered some of Lamarck's ideas as "nonsense." But at that time, Lamarck's work was not fully appreciated. Paleontologists have become aware of the value of Lamarck's service to evolution only recently.

While the early study of dinosaurs unquestionably benefitted greatly from the work of Lamarck and Cuvier, there were several other pioneers in paleontology whose work concerned the study of dinosaurs more directly.

Besides Sir Richard Owen, who coined the word dinosaur, other early English paleontologists included Gideon A. Mantell (1790–1852), William Buckland (1784–1856), Harry Govier Seeley (1839–1909), and one Englishwoman, Mary Anning (1799–1847).

Cuvier died in 1832, three years after Lamarck. Sir Richard Owen inherited the mantle of leadership in paleontology. Owen and other paleontologists in Great Britain had been following carefully the work of Cuvier and Lamarck in France, and Smith and Hutton in their own country.

The study of dinosaurs evolved from British and French paleontology. British fossil hunters had developed a highly disciplined science, amassing huge collections which were available for study in all the great universities. Most British paleontologists were originally trained in either medicine or zoology.

The story of dinosaurs really began in Great Britain in about 1824. In that year, William Buckland described a giant fossil lizard, which he named *Megalosaurus,* meaning giant lizard. It surpassed the size even of the large Meuse lizard which Baron Cuvier had classified. Cuvier himself estimated Buckland's lizard to have been at least forty feet long. The skeleton was incomplete, and a considerable amount of guessing accompanied the description of Megalosaurus.

Both Buckland and Cuvier were catastrophists, but Cuvier was considerably more cautious. While Buckland was quick to cite this lizard as a victim of the Great Deluge, Cuvier did not speculate on it, and he doubted a worldwide deluge. He favored the idea that not just one but several smaller deluges took place, and he did not guess at the causes. Buckland, on the other hand, freely mixed geology and Scripture.

When one of Cuvier's papers on natural catastrophes was obtained by Buckland, he rewrote the paper to give it a different meaning. It then read as if Cuvier himself believed in the Great Deluge. Copyright infringement being rather common in those days, Buckland now had a famous source that supported the Scripture and made his position more popular to the devout Christians among his English readers. Buckland could now say that even in England there was proof of the Great Deluge: here was a huge reptile that met its doom in the flooding of ancient England. Nineteenth-century dinosaur studies were full of these kinds of expositions.

In 1832, Gideon Mantell found the fossil remains of another giant lizard. He discovered this one in southern England. It was thought to have been armed with huge scale plates. Mantell named it *Hylaeosaurus* (hy-lee-uh-SAWR-us), meaning forest lizard.

Thus, by 1841, the fossils of four giant lizards were known. All were incomplete skeletons. They were Cuvier's mosasaur, the Iguanodon (the one which Cuvier had at first identified as a rhinoceros), the Hylaeosaurus (also discovered by Mantell), and Buckland's Megalosaurus. It should be noted that Cuvier had added his opinion to help identify these animal fossils. But because Cuvier was swayed by the similarities he noted between the three English-discovered fossils and that of the huge mosasaur (Meuse lizard), he was inclined to cast all four creatures in the same general category—they were reptilelike prehistoric lizards. As we shall see, this greatly influenced the future of dinosaur studies.

By 1841, several large collections of fossils were available for study in Europe and America. In these collections were the incomplete remains of at least nine different kinds of lizardlike prehistoric animals. Included in this group were the three giant lizards of Mantell and Buckland, and Cuvier's mosasaur. Although most paleontologists agreed that all nine of them were reptiles, a few did not agree that they were all lizards.

Sir Richard Owen was one of those who very early disagreed. He respected Cuvier's opinion, but he could not accept lumping all these animals together as lizards. He did not dispute that they were reptiles, however. What bothered Owen most about some of them was their size. The size of the fossils indicated massive animals, with lengths of up to thirty or forty feet—far too large for lizards, even giant lizards. That size would have posed mechanical and forage problems for an animal of lizardlike characteristics, assuming they were like the modern lizard. There were other features, too, that Sir Richard thought quite unlikely for lizards.

The modern lizard is a reptile. The reptiles have many characteristics in common that can be seen only by an expert zoologist (or a herpetologist—a person who specializes in handling reptiles). But they also have other less obscure characteristics—some that anyone can quickly identify. For example, they lay eggs, generally have hairless, leatherlike skin, and are *ectothermic*—they have a temperature inside the body that moves up and down according to the temperature outside the body. The common expression we use is "cold-blooded," but that is misleading and incorrect, as we shall discover when we consider the dinosaurs as reptiles.

The inclusion of the nine then existing fossils in the class of reptiles would, of course, give to them the traits that we attribute to reptiles. But we have no proof at all that modern reptiles and prehistoric reptiles are the same. It was a studied guess that prompted Owen to agree that all nine might have been reptiles.

After long deliberation, Owen became convinced that the three Mantell and Buckland lizards differed from all the others, and yet could be reptiles. He decided to regard the three as belonging to a new group of reptiles, and he proceeded to name them.

He took the Greek words *deinos,* meaning terrible, and *saurus,* meaning lizard, and formed *dinosaur*—terrible lizard.

Owen proposed the name dinosaur at a meeting of the British Association for the Advancement of Science, at Plymouth, England, August 2, 1841. His proposal was read from the world's first scientific paper on dinosaurs.

From that date, dinosaurs came into existence.

CHAPTER 3

The Study of Dinosaurs in the United States

Early American paleontologists include Caspar Wistar (1761–1818), Edward Hitchcock (1793–1864), Joseph Leidy (1823–1897), Edward Cope (1840–1897), and Othniel C. Marsh (1831–1899).

The study of dinosaurs in the United States dates from October 5, 1787, just three months after the ratification of the United States Constitution. On that date, Dr. Caspar Wistar of the American Philosophical Society presented a report at Philadelphia on a fossil discovered at Woodbury Creek, Gloucester County (near Camden), New Jersey. This fossil has been lost, but there is good evidence that it was from a large, duck-billed dinosaur. See page 103.

In 1806, William Clark of the Lewis and Clark Expedition, in Montana found and described what was probably a dinosaur fossil. That too was lost. Finally, a number of fossils turned up at a site in the Connecticut River valley in 1818. These were described at first as the remains of human beings, but later examinations determined that the bones were of a Triassic period dinosaur that lived some 200 million years ago.

From such weak beginnings, American paleontology grew, hampered at first by religious opposition.

In about 1850, paleontology received some timely aid from a change in the attitude of many people regarding geological facts and religion. Very gradually, from mid-century onward, many educated persons adopted a curious neutralism.

When Bible interpretations disputed geological data, the religious views were often laid aside or held in abeyance. The public flocked to great museums to view evidence of prehistoric life and to learn about evolution and the story of the earth as discovered and read in the rocks.

Paleontology expanded very rapidly after the publication of Darwin's theory of evolution in 1859. Paleontologists everywhere wasted little time in agreeing with Charles Darwin (1809–1882), for his ideas helped to explain a great number of mysteries regarding the appearance and disappearance of many forms of life over long periods of time. Darwin's conclusions were based on the assumption that enormous quantities of time had passed.

Physical geologists joined with Darwin, the paleontologists, and historical geologists to initiate an explosive period of growth in the life and earth sciences. This growth came between 1870 and 1920.

The spectacular late nineteenth-century flowering of dinosaur studies was due almost as much to a breakthrough in technology as it was to Darwinian biology.

Photography, invented in the late 1830s, came into use after 1850 for recording the positions of fossils in the rocks and sites of discovery. Photos replaced sketches and drawings, which were tedious and time consuming to execute. Photography reduced the possibility of errors in drawings. Private and public collections grew rapidly, but there was a great deal of confusion and controversy regarding the true nature of the fossils.

A large volume of drawings of dinosaur footprints was

published by Edward Hitchcock in 1848, but Hitchcock, who for thirteen years had collected the rocks containing these tracks, was convinced that they were made by giant birds. We now know that most of the footprints were made by Triassic period dinosaurs.

Up to 1858, no dinosaur had been definitely identified in North America. All the specimens up to this time carried some doubt with them. Some fossils, such as Hitchcock's footprints, have since been proven to be those of dinosaurs. In December 1858, Joseph Leidy described a partial skeleton of a duck-billed dinosaur at the University of Pennsylvania in Philadelphia. Also in 1858, Dr. Ferdinand Vandiveer Hayden (1829–1887), a geologist, submitted fossil teeth of several dinosaurs.

An attempt to stimulate interest in dinosaurs was made by the New York City park comptroller (commissioner) in 1868. He planned an exhibit of dinosaurs. However, before the exhibit was completed, Boss Tweed (William M. Tweed, 1823–1878, the leader of a notoriously corrupt political organization) gained control of that city's government. One of Tweed's first actions was to kill the exhibit project. In Tweed's opinion, such creatures were inventions, not science.

Had it not been for several concerned industrialists, such as Andrew Carnegie (1835–1919) and George Peabody (1795–1869), and the colorful and enterprising activities of a number of paleontologists, the American study of dinosaurs would have declined.

A rash of scientific papers appeared. The number of papers issued grew into the thousands annually by the end of the century. Some especially active paleontologists presented more than a thousand papers during their careers.

Among the outstanding paleontologists of the post–Civil War era, when dinosaurs began to be popular attractions, were Edward Cope and Othniel C. Marsh. They did much to popularize dinosaurs through their competitive fossil-collecting expeditions. Cope and Marsh had conflicting personalities which led to a continuous series of disputes. These lasted from 1868 to 1888. During their careers, Cope and Marsh published over 1,000 monographs and other works in paleontology. They are credited with the discovery of an incredible number of new fossils. For example, before Cope and Marsh began their rival careers, there were just nine types of dinosaurs known in North America. Then, in rapid succession, and in a brief twenty-year span, Cope added fifty-six new species, while Marsh discovered eighty.

After the careers of Cope and Marsh, American paleontology became international in scope and merged with European scholarship in worldwide efforts to discover the ancient past. By the early twentieth century, all the modern means of travel and most of the modern communications media were in existence. Science became a truly international discipline, and the story of dinosaurs is continued here in that spirit.

CHAPTER 4

The Modern Development of Dinosaur Studies

When the nineteenth century opened, no one had ever heard of dinosaurs. But by 1900, most of the world's present rich collections were on display in great museums in all the major cities of America and Europe. It is a high tribute to mostly French, British, and American nineteenth-century paleontologists that much of the classification work, some of the theoretical work, and many of the reconstructions have stood the challenge of review by twentieth-century scientists using their sophisticated technology. The weakness in early science is not that of people, but of their technology.

Throughout most of the nineteenth century, scientific instruments were somewhat primitive. Reliable laboratory methods were not yet fully developed. Paleontology was often rocked by argumentation, personality conflict, heated discussions, and a lot of speculation and guesswork. Mounds of new fossils accumulated in schools and laboratories all over the world. A long list of conflicting theories, hypotheses, and ideas were generated by studies of the new fossils.

Journalists, artists, and writers from educational institutions and from the press often jumped into paleontological discussions, adding to the din of controversy.

41

Many persons, both in and out of science, made strong defensive arguments in favor of some theories that were soon discredited. Unfortunately, many of these supporters found themselves in possession of obsolete books and articles, some of which they themselves produced.

Some arguments that arose in the field were continued in the schools and laboratories, often for many years thereafter.

Since dinosaurs were extinct, disputes were inevitable. There were no live specimens on which to base any reconstruction. Because no one knew what they looked like in real life, giving shape and form to them was often an exercise in imagination, and the reconstruction of a dinosaur often called for as much artistic ability as it did scientific data. The latter was often missing altogether.

Paleontologists often disagreed on the finer details of a reconstruction, such as color and type of skin. But these matters were less serious. The worst arguing took place over general structural concepts, such as the idea that some dinosaurs looked like giant lizards, or that some resembled huge kangaroos, or four-footed, prehistoric rhinoceros-type beasts. Sometimes a particular dinosaur was reconstructed along all three of those lines at different times and by different paleontologists.

Another major cause of disagreement during the nineteenth century was the scarcity of complete skeletons, and the existence of many badly damaged or poorly collected fossils. These gave rise to doubts as to age, shape, or structure, especially when such fossils were the only available specimens representing a particular animal.

After about 1875, paleontologists began to take accurate notes at the sites of discovery and to adopt safer means for recovering the fossils and transporting them without damage to laboratories.

Before these improvements were adopted, disputed dates,

inaccurate identifications, ruined fossils, and frayed tempers were the almost certain aftermath of many expeditions.

By about 1913, the great era of dinosaur hunting was over. Coincidentally, at this time, there began a new industry—motion pictures—that was to sow seeds of skepticism and introduce to the public an enormous volume of misinformation about paleontology.

By having people and dinosaurs together, the movies compounded conceptual errors with anachronism—they often mixed events and things of different ages, showing them out of their proper time and place. Dinosaurs died out some 60 million years before there were any people.

The public's respect and interest in pure science also suffered during the years between the two world wars. Soon dinosaurs came to be regarded as dead-end animals, evolutionary failures. Compounding this state of opinion was the inability of paleontologists to achieve agreement on the shape and form of dinosaurs. They were still regarded as lizards. Even their inclusion as reptiles was bad for their image.

During the first half of the twentieth century, dinosaurs were treated as forms of entertainment. People still flocked to museums, but there was little inclination on the part of scholars to question the prevailing idea that dinosaurs were failures.

This attitude was to change quickly shortly after World War II. The manner in which the study of dinosaurs changed is a remarkable chapter in the history of modern science.

After World War II, military science and hardware were freed from the grim destructive functions that had left much of the civilized world in a shambles. Nuclear physics, geophysics, space science, sonar, radar, computer electronics, metallurgical wonders, automatic guidance and tracking systems, rocketry, and jet propulsion are a few of the sophisticated weapons and technological advancements that were generated by war needs and then were freed for peaceful uses in 1945.

Scientific institutions lost no time in commandeering where possible any and all of this hardware and technology. Oceanography was among the leading disciplines to benefit from military science. Oceanography and related sciences expanded rapidly during the 1950s. It was in oceanography that some of the greatest surprises in the history of science began to turn up.

Although the main thrust of oceanographic research had little to do with dinosaurs, there were marine biologists, paleontologists, and historical geologists involved along the periphery of the oceanographic drama. These workers did see a connection between dinosaurs and what oceanographers were turning up in their research. The new data that came out of this work snowballed into nearly every other discipline, and like a giant sea wave, nearly everyone in science was overtaken by the excitement and controversy that arose from the work. For better or for worse, scientists were caught up in the widening circle of discovery, dialogue, theorizing, and finally, revision. The hallmark of the late 1960s and the decade of the 1970s was revision.

In order to make clearer just what revisions were made necessary by the new developments in science, it will be an advantage to have a bird's-eye view of earth history up to the time the dinosaurs first appeared. Since this book is not a text in historical geology, we will concentrate only on the main sequence of events in biology, leading along the path of evolution to the dinosaurs. After we have done this and have reached the time of the dinosaurs, we can then introduce elements of the new global geology as it has become recently organized (in the late 1970s). Then we will see just how much revision had to be introduced into what we know about dinosaurs and about the world in which they lived.

CHAPTER 5

The World before Dinosaurs

The earth was already an ancient planet when dinosaurs appeared, about 200 million years ago. The dinosaurs were an advanced form of life whose origins lay far backward in time—more than 3 billion years in fact.

When life first appeared on this planet it was simple and microscopically small; it lived only in the oceans. The earth's early atmosphere was made up mostly of poisonous gases. There was at first no oxygen, which is necessary to the survival of most living things. There were no plants or soil covering the rocks.

The first organisms were so simple in form that they had no mouth, no arms or legs, and did not move about in search of food. They were mostly single-cell creatures, dependent upon the chance passing of chemical food directly through the cell walls.

Such primitive creatures left no definite fossils, but they did leave evidence of their existence. There are chemicals in ancient rocks which could have gotten there only through the interaction and functioning of living things. The first definite remains of life appear in rocks about 3.2 billion years old. These remains are of a type of plant known as blue-green algae. This algae was so common that its fossil remains form layers of rock material which are called *stromatolites*. After the first plants appeared, oxygen became available for animals to breathe, because plants use the sun's energy to break down water and the gas carbon dioxide (CO_2) to liberate oxygen.

Therefore, the appearance of plants on the earth was a sure sign that animals, too, were evolving. However, from the time the first plants appeared (about 3.2 billion years ago) to the first evidence of animal life, there is a gap of over 1 billion years! During all this time, animals were undoubtedly evolving, dividing into many different kinds, and spreading out to occupy many kinds of watery environments—shallow lagoons, rocky bottoms, deep basins, etc. There was as yet not enough oxygen in the atmosphere to permit occupation of the land surface by any form of life, plant or animal.

Finally, about 600 million years ago, animals began to evolve into types that had skeletons, shells, or other hard parts. When this happened, they began to leave fossil evidence of themselves. From this point on the story of life was easier to read from the rocks.

The whole span of time from the beginning of the earth—perhaps 8 or 9 billion years ago—to the time when animals began to leave fossils in the rocks—is called the *Cryptozoic* (crip-toh-zoh-ick) eon. The name comes from the Greek *crypto,* meaning "hidden," and *zoic,* meaning "life." Hence, the term means "hidden life"—an appropriate name for this eon.

The Cryptozoic eon covers about 85 percent of the total history of the planet. But what is more important is that throughout this entire span of time, not one single event can be dated. Therefore the eon cannot be subdivided as we have been able to do with the eon that came after it.

The spiral graph shown here gives an indication of how long the Cryptozoic eon was, compared to the rest of geologic

EARTH'S TIME SPIRAL

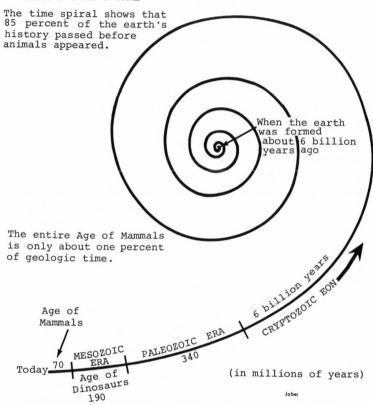

The time spiral shows that 85 percent of the earth's history passed before animals appeared.

When the earth was formed about 6 billion years ago

The entire Age of Mammals is only about one percent of geologic time.

Age of Mammals

Today 70

MESOZOIC ERA

Age of Dinosaurs 190

PALEOZOIC ERA 340

6 billion years

CRYPTOZOIC EON

(in millions of years)

Jaber

time. All we can say for sure is that life appeared, evolved into the plant and animal kingdoms, and very slowly changed from simple unicellular creatures to more complex organisms. A few soft-bodied fossils are known from the last part of the Cryptozoic eon, enough to permit scientists to detect that the most complex animals of this whole eon were ancestral forms of what we now know as worms, crustaceans, mollusks, sponges, and corals. There were no higher animals than these, and plants were mostly the small, primitive algae—non-flowering, nonbranching, and with no leaves.

The new eon, which began about 600 million years ago, and the one in which we now live, is called the *Phanerozoic* (fan-er-uh-ZOH-ick) eon. It is from the Greek too, being made up from *phanero*, meaning "visible," and the word *zoic*.

It is named for the obvious reason that, compared to the Cryptozoic eon, life is no longer hidden. But life was still quite simple, compared to today. When the Phanerozoic eon began, the most complex animal on the earth was the crablike *trilobite*, a marine *arthropod* (the class of animals to which crabs, lobsters, insects, and spiders belong). Trilobites ruled the world.

One other important difference exists between the new Phanerozoic eon and the old Cryptozoic. Many events in nature and physical happenings (mountain-building, continent-moving, ocean-forming events) could be dated, or at least placed in a sequence of time that made a more or less continuous record of earth history, beginning about 600 million years ago.

The Phanerozoic eon has been divided into three major subdivisions called *eras*, based on very large, revolutionary trends in the history of living things. The eras are the *Paleozoic*, from the Greek *paleo*, meaning "ancient," and *zoic*, meaning "life"; *Mesozoic*, meaning "middle life," and *Cenozoic*, "recent life." See the Geologic Time Chart.

The Paleozoic era started at the beginning of the Phanerozoic eon and lasted 345 million years. The era is subdivided on the basis of major biological and geological events into seven *periods*. The first period is the *Cambrian*, named for the highlands in Wales where rocks of this period were first discovered. The Cambrian lasted 80 million years. Animals were still primitive; mostly bottom-feeding, mud-burrowing animals, and a few types that floated in the water at various levels. Trilobites were the rulers, but none of them achieved a size larger than a foot or two across. There were no land

Geologic Time Chart

EON	ERA	PERIOD	EPOCH	Radiometric dates in millions of years from the present	Duration in millions of years	Physical Events	Life Events
PHANEROZOIC EON	Cenozoic Era	QUATERNARY	Pleistocene	2	2	Ice Age	Human beings
		TERTIARY (Age of Mammals)	Pliocene	12	10	Colorado River begins	Mammals take over
			Miocene	23	11		
			Oligocene	35	12	Antarctica and Australia split from each other and move away	
			Eocene	57	22		
			Paleocene	70	13		Dinosaurs gone
	Mesozoic Era	CRETACEOUS	(Age of Dinosaurs / Age of Reptiles)	145	75	Mississippi River begins / Atlantic Ocean begins to form as narrow ribbon of water	(Age of Dinosaurs / Age of Mammals appear)
		JURASSIC		210	65	Continental Drift begins	
		TRIASSIC		260	50	Pangaea Rifting / Climates are drier	Flowering Plants and birds
	Paleozoic Era	PERMIAN	(Age of Amphibians)	315	55	Appalachian Mountains formed	Dinosaurs begin / Conifers
		CARBONIFEROUS — PENNSYLVANIAN		345	30	Ancient continents of Laurasia and Gondwana formed, but may have been joined earlier in giant super continent of Pangaea	Reptiles begin / Great Swamp forests
		CARBONIFEROUS — MISSISSIPPIAN		385	40		Amphibians rule the world
		DEVONIAN	Age of Fishes	440	55	Climates are mild	Forests begin / Insects appear
		SILURIAN	(Age of Invertebrates)	465	25	Ancient proto-Atlantic Ocean formed and then destroyed in formation of supercontinent of Pangaea	Plants appear on dry land
		ORDOVICIAN		520	55		Marine invertebrates are the highest form of life
		CAMBRIAN		600	80	Climates are tropical or subtropical nearly everywhere / Days are much shorter / Oxygen level too low for life / No land animals or plants	

Age of Dinosaurs / Age of Reptiles during this part of the earth's history.

Epochs can be distinguished only roughly and locally during this part of the earth's history.

Passage of time is read upward on this chart.

CRYPTOZOIC EON

Precambrian Era

Jaber

plants, but plenty of plants lived in the ocean. They made up a large part of the *plankton,* or drifting food on which so many animals depended. They were the basis of the world's first food chains.

The second, or *Ordovician* period, began 520 million years ago and lasted 55 million years. It is named for an ancient people who lived in a section of Wales where rocks of Ordovician age were first discovered. This was a time of transition. Plants had begun to invade the land; the first vertebrates appeared—backboned animals. These latter were the jawless fishes. Trilobites still reigned supreme at the beginning of the Ordovician period, but at the end their place was being taken by more complex animals, such as the giant shrimplike creatures called *Eurypterids* (yoo-RIP-ter-ids). Great flooding of low-lying areas took place during the period. Climates seemed to be tropical and moist nearly everywhere.

In North America a great mountain system was pushed up slowly over a span of several million years. But during the next few periods the whole system was eroded away. The Taconic Mountains of eastern New York state are the remnants of this once-high mountain range.

The *Silurian,* shortest of all geologic periods, began 430 million years ago and lasted 30 million years. It was a time of calm. Warm climates prevailed over most of the land areas. Plants began to invade the uplands and started their evolution into many lines and groups.

But the most important biological event was not the success of plants, but of fishes. Fishes began to evolve into many branches. The main types were jawless; many had armor or plates of various kinds. Some armored and jawless fishes were very large, up to twenty or thirty feet long.

Giantism became a new evolutionary phenomeon among plants and animals. Another fearsome animal of Silurian seas was the Eurypterid, which continued from the previous period. In the Silurian period, Eurypterids developed into the largest arthropods that ever existed—some were over six feet long.

Giant scorpions, some of about the same length, shared the oceans with the Eurypterids and fishes. The scorpions may have become the first air-breathing animals, for there is some evidence that they took to the land. If so, they were the first land animals. Flying creatures, insects, and four-footed animals had not yet evolved. The world in Silurian time was still a very bleak place, at least on land.

The *Devonian* period followed. It began 400 million years ago and lasted 50 million years. It is best known as the Age of Fishes. True bony fishes—the modern fishes—developed at this time. Although climates generally remained warm, some deserts developed, too. Forests began to evolve, but they contained many types of trees that no longer exist.

Devonian fishes existed in astounding variety. Among them wer the strange crossopterygians (cross-op-ter-EE-gee-uns). These were evolving legs and lungs. They were the ancestors of all land animals. The very first amphibians appeared in the Devonian period. *Ichthyostega* (ick-thee-yoh-STAY-guh), the earliest known amphibian, had a fishlike tail and very small, weak legs. Yet from this three-foot-long animal was to evolve human beings and also the largest land animals that ever lived.

With amphibians, true land animals began to appear, taking their place among the plants which had already begun to form swamps and marshes along the coasts, and forests farther inland.

The Devonian fishes included the first sharks, many kinds of jawless fishes, plated fishes (some over thirty feet long), and the modern bony fishes. Spiders, millipedes, and freshwater clams also first appeared in Devonian times. This was truly a dynamic period in the earth's long history.

LABYRINTHODONT AMPHIBIANS

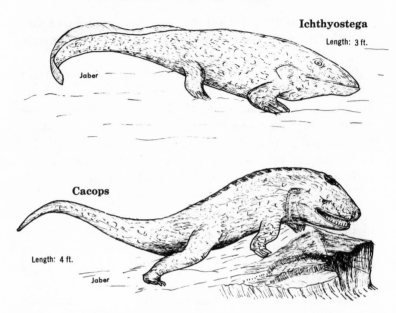

Ichthyostega

Length: 3 ft.

Jaber

Cacops

Length: 4 ft.

Jaber

Fig. 3 (top). An early labyrinthodont amphibian (Mississippian period). Its fishlike features betray the fact that it evolved from the fishes only shortly before. This is the first four-footed animal.

Fig. 3 (bottom). A much later amphibian, from the Permian period. This animal has almost no fishlike traits. It has evolved toward the reptile and has many reptile features.

It was followed by a period known as *Carboniferous* in Europe, but in America is generally subdivided into two periods: the *Mississippian* period which began 350 million years ago and lasted 40 million years; succeeded by the *Pennsylvanian* period, which began 310 million years ago and lasted 35 million years. Taken together, these two periods are known as the Age of Coal, or Age of Amphibians.

Both names are quite appropriate. Many great swamp forests existed. The climates remained moist and tropical over large areas of the earth. These forests are the source of most of the large coal fields. Coal represents the fossil remains of stems, branches, tree trunks, leaves, and plant spores. The great scale trees were the largest plants, reaching heights of over 100 feet. On the drier ground in the highlands, the first conifers and leaf trees, such as the gingko, developed. Horsetails, scouring rushes, seed ferns, true ferns, and fern trees were growing nearly everywhere. Insects first appeared in great variety and numbers toward the end of the Mississippian.

Amphibians continued to develop new varieties. They grew in size and spread to all the land areas. Amphibians ruled the world during these two periods. But the animals that were to dethrone them—the reptiles—had already appeared.

The reptiles first appeared early in the Pennsylvanian period, about 300 million years ago. The earliest types were all very small and lizardlike. Their ability to spread out, evolve new kinds, and conquer the earth was due principally to one major innovation: they developed an egg with a tough outer membrane, enclosed within a leathery shell. This egg resisted drying and provided a complete life-support unit for the reptile embryo. Unlike the amphibian which always had to

Cotylosaur
(Stem reptile)

Jaber

Length: 5 ft.

Fig. 4. The first true reptile. This is *Limnocleis,* a cotylosaur of the Pennsylvanian period. Its general shape and form resembles that of Cacops in Fig. 3.

return to water to lay their eggs, reptiles could lay their eggs on dry land. The young were born as miniature adults, ready to fight and capture their food in a fiercely competitive world. The first reptiles were meat-eating animals.

Although reptiles had arrived, they remained less important than amphibians throughout the Carboniferous period and into the following period, the *Permian*.

The Permian period brought the Paleozoic era to an end. Widespread extinctions closed out the era, taking a heavy toll on the number and kinds of animals. New kinds of animals developed, however, to replace those that failed to survive the changes. Climates cooled off; mountain ranges were elevated; volcanism increased; and the world's land and water became redistributed, mainly by means of *continental drift*. (See Chapter 6.) Ancient shallow seas drained off the land as it rose above sea level. Finally, large areas of the earth were subjected to an ice age, and there appeared to be an increase in deserts as compared to the calm period that preceded the Permian.

CHAPTER 6

The New Global Geology and Continental Drift

Having traced the evolution of life from its simplest forms in the very distant past up to the arrival of reptiles on the scene, about 225 million years ago, we can now pursue our original aim of introducing elements of the new global geology and see what bearing it has on the development of dinosaurs. It is absolutely necessary to understand some basic concepts in global geology in order to comprehend what happened to the dinosaurs.

It was noted in the last chapter that the Permian period contained so many dramatic changes, both in the evolution of life and in the history of the planet, that it brought the Paleozoic era to a close. A new world of living things dawned. Gone were whole groups of common animals both on land and in the seas.

A time of deep crisis overtook all living things. Drastic changes took place in climates and environments and in the shape, location, and contour of the land. Changes were also found in the size, form, and depth of oceans.

When the curtain rises again—when the Great Dying is over—and count is taken as recorded in the fossil record, we see that amphibians were greatly reduced in the number of groups surviving. Likewise, the very large group of mammal-like reptiles, comprising 170 genera in the Permian, was reduced to only 17 genera at the end of the period. Other groups of reptiles took their places. More than 80 new types appeared toward the end of the period. Among these new reptiles were the *thecodonts* (see fig. 9), the ancestors of dinosaurs.

The Age of Reptiles had dawned, and with it a new era of life. What could have happened during the 50 million years of the Permian period to bring about such dramatic changes? Until recently, nothing more than an educated guess could be offered as an answer to this question.

A similar time of worldwide changes had occurred 600 million years ago, to begin the Paleozoic era, and another one occurred just 70 million years ago to end the Age of Dinosaurs and bring on our present era (the *Cenozoic*, which is known as the Age of Mammals). In fact, less extensive periods of change, often accompanied by crises in animal life, have been used to mark off the geologic periods, including the six periods we have discussed already in our survey of the Paleozoic era.

In the 1970s, following revolutionary discoveries in oceanography and geophysics, some of the answers began to turn up.

The story of these discoveries began between 1925 and 1927. Depth measurements revealed the existence of a long, winding, submerged ridge in the Atlantic Ocean. In the next few years this ridge was traced throughout its extent, and it was discovered to continue from the Atlantic into the Indian Ocean around Africa. Simultaneously, seismologists (earthquake scientists) began to notice that earthquakes occurred more often along this submerged ridge than anywhere else. World War II interrupted the research and study of this strange, earth-girdling feature.

Shortly after the war, a dramatic discovery relating to the Mid-Atlantic Ridge was made by a young woman, Marie Tharp, who was compiling a seafloor profile, using depth data provided by various research ships. Tharp noticed that her tracings across the Mid-Atlantic Ridge showed a dip at the top of the ridge. This dip always appeared wherever her tracing crossed the ridge. She interpreted this dip as a rift— a deep canyon in the middle of the ridge. She later saw that this canyon followed the entire course of the ridge. Later discoveries by other workers showed that other submerged ridges also contained this unique rift.

By the late 1950s, the worldwide network of ridges had been revealed—it was 40,000 miles long (65,000 kilometers) and almost encircled some continents. From this discovery, it was not long before several workers in oceanography had deduced the meaning of the great undersea mountain network: the ridge was the boundary between gigantic moving blocks of the earth's outer crust. These blocks, later named plates, carried continents and parts of ocean basins on them.

Wherever the plate boundaries were located, there was always earthquake activity. Scientists in the 1970s were finally able to record movement. Some of the plates were moving at speeds of two to four inches per year. That is not very much movement, but over a period of a few million years it is enough to completely alter the earth's surface.

The second major discovery, made almost simultaneously, was that the seafloor in all the oceans was not more than 150 million years old at any point. What happened to the ancient seafloor of the Paleozoic era?

The answer to this question involves yet another major discovery: the founding of deep-sea trenches. These are always distant from and opposite to the ridges, and they, too, were discovered to be seismically active—earthquakes were very frequent and often very strong under the trenches.

The riddle of ridges, trenches, and plates was solved between 1962 and 1972. The solution entailed the revival of the *Continental Drift theory,* first devised in 1912, and advocated by the German meteorologist, Alfred Wegener (1880–1930). Wegener believed that one reason why Africa's western coast appeared to fit against South America's eastern coast was that they were actually united at one time in the distant past.

Wegener cited the similarities between ancient plants and animals in South America and Africa as proof that these two continents were once joined together. Fossils of plants and animals have been used extensively since Wegener's time to support and strengthen the theory of Continental Drift. The jigsaw puzzle fit, and the relationships in ancient fauna and flora were the major evidence offered during Wegener's lifetime. If that had been the only body of supportive data, the theory of Continental Drift would not have been revived. "Drifters," or supporters of that theory, received a large accumulation of new evidence after World War II.

We have already cited the supportive evidence contained in the discovery and study of the mid-ocean undersea mountain network, the ridge rift, the trenches, and the seemingly harmonious idea of plates. Between 1962 and 1972, these studies were molded into the complex theory of *Seafloor Spreading,* which then gave rise to the new science of *Plate Tectonics.* The theory of Seafloor Spreading brought together all the discovered elements—the sea trenches, plates, and ridges—into a unified exposition of how the earth's crust was breaking up, moving about, rejoining, and breaking up again, in continuous motion, at the rate of just a few inches per year.

The earth's crust is brittle and varies in thickness from about five miles thick below the oceans to about forty miles thick under the continents. The crust rides on a layer called the *mantle.* The mantle rock is so hot that it would flow like a liquid except that the pressure of rock above it keeps it in a solid state. But the crust of the earth is not in one piece.

There are at least twelve large plates. Some, like the Nazca Plate in the Pacific Ocean, are entirely covered by water, while others, such as the Africa Plate, consist of a continent and parts of the surrounding oceans.

Some plates are moving apart, some are colliding, and others are moving past each other. The famous San Andreas Fault in California is really the edges of two plates moving past each other. They are the Pacific Plate, which is slowly moving southeastward, and the North America Plate, which is moving past it in a northwest direction. The city of Los Angeles lies on the Pacific Plate and is moving northwestward a few inches per year. In a few million years, Los Angeles will be at the same latitude that San Francisco is now. The latter city is on the North America Plate and is moving southeastward.

The two plates are moving so slowly that movement takes place in periodic slippages. The last major slip was in 1906, which destroyed much of the city of San Francisco. When these slippages are going to occur is now a topic of intense research—an effort to warn big-city dwellers of impending disaster. The slippages occur as shallow earthquakes.

Earthquakes are more common at plate boundaries than anywhere else. They are simply the evidence of movement between two plates. In the 1970s scientists have finally been able to measure the actual movement between two plates.

PROVING CONTINENTAL DRIFT. Wegener had no knowledge of what the force was that broke up the crust into gigantic slabs and moved it about. After all, the crust is solid rock and weighs billions of tons per square mile of surface. But he and other scientists speculated on it. Up until about 1932, no one could give an answer that was satisfactory to more than a few colleagues.

Actually, Wegener had a germ of an idea that later proved

to be very close to what is today considered to be the force that moves great continents. Wegener's tragic death on a Greenland icecap in 1930 left it to others to work out. Sir Arthur Holmes, a British geologist, picked up Wegener's idea and developed it.

Wegener had speculated that maybe some kind of convection current was the force being sought. Holmes agreed. He viewed the earth's surface like the surface of boiling water in a pot on a stove. Boiling water moves from the bottom of the pot, up the sides, across the top surface, and then down the opposite side to the bottom again, where it mixes and prepares to repeat the process.

Holmes's convection current idea looked good in theory. But World War II intervened, and the idea was laid aside. By 1960, the entire network of undersea ridges was known, as were most of those mysterious deep-sea trenches, which were to figure so prominently in the revival of the Continental Drift theory.

It was Harry H. Hess, then of Princeton University, who, in 1960, put Holmes's theory to work. First, he used it to explain the ridges, then the deep-sea trenches, and finally he arrived at a bold new view of the earth's geologic past.

Hess said that lava wells up from deep within the earth, riding up on huge convection currents. It cracks open the crust at the mid-ocean ridges and wedges in, pushing the two sides apart. The lava solidifies to become rock and is incorporated into the ocean floor. As more lava comes up, it pushes the older rock outward and away on both sides of the ridge. The original rock moves farther and farther away from the ridge. Where is the rock going? There is no space for it unless the earth's crust expands. But there is no evidence that the earth is getting larger.

The explanation that Hess gave is that the old rock—the rock farthest from the ridge—is sucked back down into the earth and destroyed. It is remelted. Where does this happen? Hess pointed to the great oceanic trenches as the place where the ocean floor is being slowly destroyed.

He noted that trenches lie opposite and away from the mid-ocean ridges; around and under the trenches earthquakes are numerous, often violent, and occur very deep in the rocks.

The ocean floor moves along after it is formed at the mid-ocean ridge. Continents, which are made of lighter rock, ride along on top of this floor, like groceries on a conveyor belt. But when the floor that carries a continent on it reaches a trench, it gets rid of at least part of the lighter rocks of the continent. As the ocean floor slips down into the mantle, the continental rock is crushed and crunched up at the back side of the trench. The continental rock piles up to form a mountain range at the back edge. The Andes range of South America is one example of a mountain system being created today as a seafloor goes down a trench. The trench in this case is the deep Peru Trench, and it is the site where the Nazca Plate is being destroyed.

Robert S. Dietz of the Environmental Science Services Administration named Hess's work the theory of Seafloor Spreading. Two other scientists who quickly saw the merit in the Hess theory provided crucial support to the theory from an entirely new source—*geomagnetism.*

The original ideas that led to linking up the Continental Drift theory with geomagnetism were mainly those of a Nobel prize winner, Patrick M. S. Blackett (1897–1974), an English physicist. According to Blackett and his colleagues, the earth has a giant magnetic field. The lines of force of this magnetic field enter the earth at the North Magnetic Pole. They course through the earth and leave it at the South Magnetic Pole. These poles are located near but do not coincide with the geographic north and south poles. A compass needle

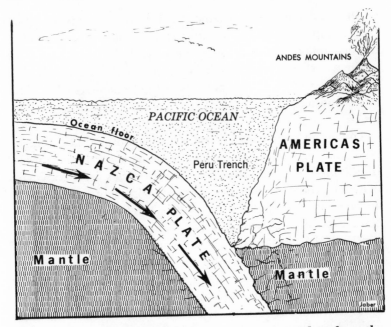

Fig. 5. This diagram shows what is happening today along the western coast of South America, particularly off the coast of Chile. The Pacific Ocean floor (the Nazca Plate) is being destroyed very slowly—a few inches per year. It is moving down into the hot mantle rock under the Americas Plate. This movement accounts for severe earthquakes and volcanoes, and is responsible for creating the gigantic Andes Mountains chain.

will point straight down at the Magnetic North Pole and straight up at the Magnetic South Pole. This is how the two poles are located, since right at the poles are the only places on earth where the lines of force enter and leave.

But a compass needle is not the only thing that can record the direction of the lines of force in the earth's magnetic field. Molten rock or pottery clay in a kiln will record the direction of the lines. These substances contain metallic matter which is affected by natural magnetism. The particles of metallic matter in molten rock (lava) or in hot, melted pottery clay in a kiln align themselves in the direction of the earth's magnetic field. They become a weak magnet themselves.

When the lava or pottery clay cools and solidifies, this alignment becomes permanent and will never change—even for millions of years—as long as the rock or pottery is not remelted.

Here is the key to record any movement in the earth's crust in the past. In 1954, Blackett and other workers discovered that the lines of force in the magnetic field had changed direction in the past, and the changes were recorded in any molten rock that happened to be lying around at the time the change occurred.

When young rocks were studied it was noted that their permanent magnetic alignment was the same as that of the actual alignment of the magnetic field today. But as older rocks were measured, the lines of force were seen to have been in a different direction from the present. The difference increased in still older rocks. This could only mean that the direction in which the rocks lay had changed. In other words, the whole area had moved.

Geologists soon discovered that even the Magnetic North Pole and Magnetic South Pole had wandered in a definite path over several million years.

But the biggest surprise came when scientists on different continents found that the path described by the wandering Magnetic North Pole was different on each continent. This could only mean the existence of two or more pairs of magnetic poles (that is, two or more Magnetic South poles and two or more Magnetic North poles)—an impossibility.

Scientists were mystified until someone thought of cutting up a map to eliminate the Atlantic Ocean, and thus move

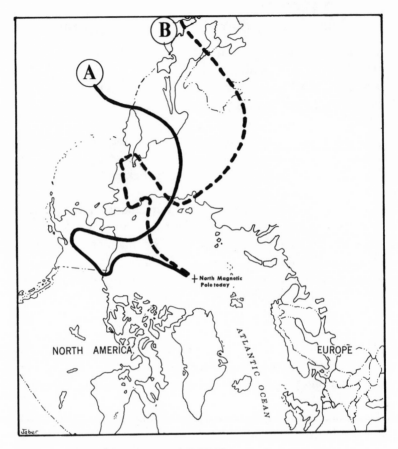

Fig. 6. THE WANDERING POLE

Measurement of paleomagnetism to prove that the continents have moved.

"A" marks the path of the North Magnetic Pole as it has moved during the past 300 million years, as measured in the rocks of *Europe*.

"B" is the path as measured in the rocks of *North America* for the same time period. If the Atlantic Ocean were taken out and the two continents pushed together, the two paths would coincide and become one. This proves that there was no Atlantic Ocean 300 million years ago.

Europe, North America, Africa, and South America all together to form one giant supercontinent. There was the solution—the pairs of poles disappeared, and instead, we find one path, proving that each of the continents had been wandering. A giant supercontinent had existed. It had split apart and an ocean had formed in between the pieces.

Subsequent research confirmed these facts along other lines of investigation. The split had occurred near the end of the Permian period, about 300 million years ago. It is still going on, there now being over 3,000 miles separating the two western parts from the two eastern parts. Moreover, further research with magnetism has proven that Australia, India, and Antarctica were also involved.

In the 1970s a body of data began to surface that appeared to contradict in part the existence of one giant supercontinent (which was given the name *Pangaea*). The possibility exists that Pangaea was not one but two continents, separated for much of their history by an ancient sea, now called the Tethys Sea. The Tethys Sea lay approximately where the Mediterranean Sea is today. South of the Tethys Sea was Gondwanaland, comprising what is now Africa, South America, Antarctica, and Australia. Also appended to it, but splitting away and moving northward later, was the huge continental block that we now know as India.

North of the Tethys Sea was Laurasia, comprising what is now Western Europe; possibly Greenland; and much of Eastern Europe and western Asia, but not including the Arabian Peninsula (that was with Gondwanaland), and perhaps not including China, or parts of China (there is some evidence that this part of eastern Asia was also with Gondwanaland).

The location and disposition of North America in relation to Laurasia and Gondwanaland are somewhat doubtful because of conflicting theories. However, most authorities are

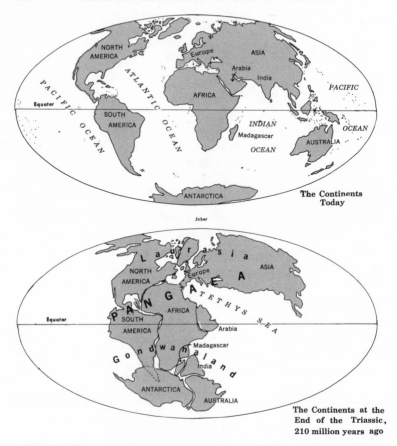

Fig. 7. The map shows the positions of the continents when dinosaurs first appeared. Note that they could reach any continent by walking on land. This accounts for the remarkable similarities between dinosaurs on different continents. For example, some North American sauropod dinosaurs were nearly exactly like those that lived in Africa at the same time.

The breaking up of Pangaea brought on a long series of climate changes. These presented challenges to evolving animals. They met the challenge by evolving new species (types) to fit any kind of environment. This explains the great diversity of dinosaurs.

agreed that at least in the early phase, North America was attached to Africa. It was rotated so that the present Atlantic coast ran in a more east-west direction and also lay much closer to the equator than it does today. Consequently, to go from what is now New Jersey or Virginia to Morocco in Northern Africa, one had merely to walk over—as many dinosaurs undoubtedly did.

The study of geomagnetism in the past is called *paleogeomagnetism*. While the reconstruction of the ancient supercontinent was proceeding on paper during the late 1960s, a group of scientists was pursuing another avenue of research in paleogeomagnetism. In their work they hit upon a fantastic discovery that confirmed the Hess theory of how Continental Drift took place and may even have shed a ray of light on the mystery of why the dinosaurs became extinct.

The key to the discovery is an obscure fact that had been known as far back as the late nineteenth century. This fact is that some rocks are known to have been magnetized in the reverse to what was expected. That is, magnetization was pointing toward opposite poles. We would expect rocks to be magnetized at least in the general direction of the North Magnetic Pole. But instead, some rocks have a magnetization that points directly to the South Magnetic Pole—also originally regarded as an impossible situation, almost as bad as the previous dilemma of having more than one pair of magnetic poles.

Studies in 1950 showed that this situation is not impossible. The poles have indeed reversed themselves at various times in the past. The North Magnetic Pole became the South Magnetic Pole and vice versa. Furthermore, these reversals have taken place much more often in the past 70 million years than at any other time. The poles have been reversing three or four times every million years or so.

Reversal is not sudden. The magnetic field weakens very

slowly, for about 4,000 years, and then flips, perhaps several times in a few hundred years. It finally stabilizes in a reversed position and regains the original force strength.

What is important about this is that during the periods of weak magnetic field, the earth loses its protection from flying cosmic debris in the form of various rapidly moving subatomic particles—tiny bits of matter that speed along at thousands of miles per second. These "cosmic rays" are able to penetrate anything. They often go right through the earth. Many of them originate in the sun or nearby stars, and some come from great distances out in space, perhaps even from other galaxies. But they can be dangerous to life, particularly to the reproductive cells in living things.

Wild speculations are heard about the dangers from reversing polarity. However, most scientists now agree that the only way the periods of reversing polarity are harmful is in the changes in climate that they are able to bring about. The precise way in which this occurs is not a subject that should concern us here. We are more concerned with the influence that the reversing polarity discovery has had on proving Continental Drift.

In the late 1950s, it was discovered that the ocean floor is not nearly as old as other parts of the world. In fact, all the ocean floors were discovered to be relatively young, less than 150 million years in every case.

At the time this was discovered, magnetic surveys were being taken of the ocean bottoms. Extremely detailed surveys in the Pacific Ocean showed that magnetic variations in the floor occurred in narrow strips, showing that the earth's magnetism was alternately higher and lower. The strips were all about the same width—18.5 miles (30 kilometers)—and all extended for hundreds of miles between fracture zones, or areas where movement, earthquakes, and faulting were happening.

On a magnetic tape, the patterns that developed looked like the stripes of a zebra. They were very mysterious, since no one could figure out why the ocean floor could have these magnetic variations at such uniform intervals.

Then, in 1963, Harry Hess had an idea and set out to test it. It took four years. In 1967 Hess announced that the polarity changes in the ocean floor on one side of a deep sea ridge always matched those on the other side of the ridge *and had a sequence that matched the table of reversals of the earth's magnetic field!*

When Hess made this announcement, a quick check of all other oceanographic magnetic data for ridges was made. In every case, the same reversal patterns showed up. What did all this mean?

For one thing, it proved that the rocks welled up as lava, pushed up through the ridge, pushed aside older rock, and then solidified, taking on the magnetic alignment that was present at the time it came up.

The zebra stripes were separate episodes of lava flow and floor movement. Furthermore, since the exact dates of the last few reversals of the magnetic field are known, the dates of each episode in the ocean floor could be obtained, and the rate of movement could be determined.

Thus, in the 1970s we learned that North America is moving westward at about one inch per year, while the Pacific Ocean floor is moving eastward at two inches per year (about five centimeters). There is a collision going on between the Nazca Plate carrying part of the Pacific Ocean floor, and the continent of South America. The Nazca Plate is losing, since it is being *subducted,* sucked down and under the continent in the great Peru Trench. (See Fig. 5.) The collision is the cause of all the destructive earthquakes that are occurring along the western coast of South America. The Andes Mountains were created by this collision—and they are still rising.

We have proven that Continental Drift does take place and has done so in the past.

Our next task is to determine what, if any, effect Continental Drift has had upon the dinosaurs.

In order to carry on this discussion, we have to revert our attention to the end of the Permian period and continue to trace the evolution of life in the new era that followed—the *Mesozoic* era.

CHAPTER 7

The Age of Reptiles

The most important physical event of Mesozoic time which succeeded the Paleozoic era was Continental Drift—the breakup of the ancient supercontinent of Pangaea. It had probably already started cracking apart late in the Permian period of the Paleozoic era. Some scientists believe that by the time the curtain had risen on the new Mesozoic world, Pangaea had split in an east-west direction into the northern continent of Laurasia and the southern continent of Gondwanaland. These two continents were also in the early stages of breaking up.

Thus, one salient feature of the earth's history in the early Triassic period (the first period of the Mesozoic era) was change. Changes in the earth's climates, physical features, and living systems were far more rapid than they had been in the Permian period. All these changes brought on a time of crisis for every living thing.

Some of them met the challenges by evolving new varieties that adapted better to the altered conditions—different climates and new environments. Other animals tried, but failed, and either died out completely or continued on as less important, reduced in kinds and numbers.

The amphibians are among the latter. They lost considerable influence during the transition to Mesozoic time. The Age of Amphibians gave way to the Age of Reptiles. The decline of amphibians is thought to be related to their failure to shed their dependence upon water: having to return to water as adults to lay eggs and to breed. Moreover, the cooling climates resulted in a reduction of area covered by environments favorable to amphibians (swamp forests, for example).

On the other hand, the spreading of plants into the highlands and their evolution of both cool-climate and arid-climate forms favored reptiles. Reptiles moved into the new environments and filled them with animals that were better adapted to the new world they were inheriting.

EVOLUTION.   Again, let us be reminded that none of this happened overnight. It took millions of years for the changes in environments to have any effect upon plants and animals. Evolution in biology means the gradual and slow development of complex organisms from simpler ancestral forms over long periods of time.

Evolution's progress is by means of natural selection. Natural selection operates in the environment through competition for food, territory, reproduction, and defense. Any mutation in an animal or plant that tends to favor it over others of the same or competing species insures that animal or plant a better chance of living and reproducing. It can then pass on its mutated advantage to future generations. Thus, if a reptile, born with longer hind legs than is the average for the species, finds that its legs give it an advantage over its fellow reptiles, the chances are very good that this reptile will breed. The longer legs *may* be transmitted to the next generation, but there is no guarantee that it will be.

Many mutations result in the early death of an organism, too. Such mutations do not help, but rather hurt the chances for survival. In such a case, the animal or plant would not live long enough to breed and thus would fail to pass the mutation on to the next generation. An example is a bird born without feathers. If that happens, it is a mutation, and it does not help the bird to survive. It does, however, lead to the premature death of the bird, which prevents it from breeding.

Evolution proceeds in this manner, generation after generation, weeding out bad mutations and transmitting to the future the good mutations—mutations that help insure survival.

By natural selection the reptiles of the Mesozoic era evolved many successful new kinds: fast-running predators; two-legged jumpers; heavily armored grazers and browsers; agile tree climbers; great flyers and soaring specialists; gigantic, ferocious meat-eating animals; even larger, but docile, peaceful plant eaters; and finally, a whole range of swift, truly marvelous marine animals.

With these grand forces, the reptiles reached out into every earth environment and conquered it. By the middle of the era (mid-Triassic period), reptiles were the supreme rulers of the earth. When the ruling reptiles—the dinosaurs— arrived on the scene, as they did by late Triassic time, the reptile domination of the earth was complete and assured to remain that way for over 100 million years. That is far longer than the mammals have ruled. Therefore, we cannot say that dinosaurs were failures simply because they died out. We have to look at that enormous span of time in which they reigned supreme. In addition, they may not even be extinct, as we shall see when we discuss the later evolutionary trends among these animals.

In the review of Paleozoic life, it was noted that the reptiles evolved from clumsy *labyrinthodont* (lab-ee-RINTH-ohdont) amphibians. (See Fig. 3.) These roughly resembled the modern crocodiles, except that they had very snubbed noses. Hence, it is no surprise that the first reptiles were sprawling, low-slung, elongate animals. They did not have the grace nor the structural beauty of their later descendants, the dinosaurs.

The very first reptiles were the *Cotylosaurs* (KOT-ee-loh-sawrs). (See Fig. 4.) This group gave rise to so many different kinds of reptiles that scientists call them "stem" reptiles. Cotylosaurs had already developed and radiated outward into many branches by the time the Mesozoic era had begun.

A very closely related group of reptiles, the *Pelycosaurs* (PEH-lee-koh-sawrs) (also called mammallike reptiles), were developing at about the same time. The Pelycosaurs evolved seventy-eight different kinds before the Mesozoic era began. But in the great crisis of life that marks the threshold to Mesozoic time, the Pelycosaurs declined rapidly, there being only about seventeen groups left by the time the new era opened. By mid-*Jurassic* (the second period of the Mesozoic era), the Pelycosaurs were gone. But before they died out, one group evolved into the first mammals. However, mammals were to remain small and insignificant for another 100 million years.

Cotylosaurs gradually took over the world in early Triassic time. They gave rise to the turtles, snakes, lizards, and several groups of marine reptiles. From them finally evolved a small bipedal animal called a *Thecodont* (THEE-koh-dont)—the ancestor of dinosaurs and birds.

Thecodonts first appeared in early Triassic time. Most were very small reptiles, up to about three feet long. They differed from lizards outwardly by having hind legs that were longer than the front legs, and they stood up and ran on their hind legs. This bipedal tendency is one of the major traits of dinosaurs. All but a few groups of them were bipedal.

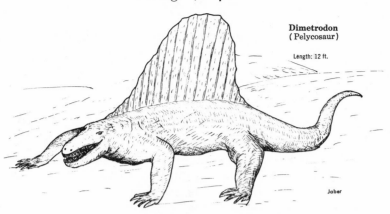

Dimetrodon
(Pelycosaur)

Length: 12 ft.

Jaber

Fig. 8. These early reptiles belonged to a group known as the pelycosaurs, which gave rise to mammal-like reptiles and to mammals. Dimetrodon was probably the largest land animal of its time—early Permian period.

The Thecodonts went through an evolutionary radiation to form many different kinds of animals. Most of this evolution occurred through the opening up of many new environments as a result of changes due to the splitting and drifting of the continents. This had begun just as the Thecodonts began their spectacular evolution.

Many Thecodont groups developed into crocodilelike animals, and some took to the air, evolving two airborne groups —the birds and the *Pterosaurs* (TER-oh-sawrs), or flying reptiles.

Dinosaurs arose in late Triassic time from swift bipedal Thecodonts with meat-eating habits, and with a well-developed skeleton that no longer resembled the lowly Cotylosaurian ancestors. Instead, Thecodonts walked erect and used their long tails for balance. Their bones became lighter and more streamlined in design. Their legs moved under, raising the body high off the ground instead of being slung from the sides in the manner of the modern crocodiles or amphibians. The front legs tended to become short, and in some groups evolved into arms with grasping hands. When running, the Thecodonts poised forward, raised their tails off the ground and loped in a light, swaying manner. When they sat down, the body rested in a vertical position against folded hind legs in kangaroo fashion.

From these animals came all the dinosaurs, great and small. There were two major divisions in the dinosaur family. The oldest and first to evolve was the *Saurischian* (sawr-is-kee-un) group. But before considering them, it is best to take a look at the basic differences between the two orders of dinosaurs.

CHAPTER 8

Dinosaurs as Reptiles

The term dinosaur refers to two distinct groups of prehistoric animals. They are about as related to each other as cows are to horses. Cows and horses belong to the class of mammals, but they are within two different orders of the class. Similarly, dinosaurs form two distinct orders within the reptile class.

What is a reptile? It is an air-breathing, egg-laying animal with hairless, leathery skin, and with an anatomy and physiology that is clearly distinguishable in many features from those of any other class of animals. The latter distinction is a matter for science, but there are internal differences between reptiles and other classes that can be detected easily by anyone.

For example, reptile young complete their birth cycle (body formation) within a tough-skinned egg. Modern reptiles are mostly *ectothermic* (see chapter 2). Mammals are *endothermic,* which means that the animal has an internal blood temperature-regulating mechanism that can maintain a steady blood temperature despite most normal weather conditions. In mammals the blood remains at or close to 100°F (39°C). Both ectothermic and endothermic animals have upper and lower temperature limits. They will die if these limits are exceeded too quickly or for too long a period of time.

On the basis of evidence amassed up to this time, dinosaurs have been included in the class of reptiles. In the matter of blood temperature, however, there are now a number of arguments against the inclusion of dinosaurs in the reptile class. But these arguments can be put aside for now, until after a full description of the dinosaurs.

Because they are reptiles, dinosaurs are considered to be closely related to lizards, snakes, turtles, and crocodiles (the latter term in science encompasses alligators, caimans, and gavials, as well as some prehistoric crocodiles).

The two groups of dinosaurs are the *Saurischians* and *Ornithischians* (or-nee-THIS-kee-uns). The *Saurischians* (sawr-IS-kee-uns) got their name because of a major distinguishing anatomical feature—their hip and pelvic anatomy. Because this anatomy resembles the hips and pelvic region of the lizards, the word *saurus* (Greek for lizard) and *ischios* (IS-kee-ohs) meaning pelvis in Greek were combined to form the name, which may be literally translated as "lizard-hip."

The Ornisthischians are similarly distinguishable by their hip and pelvic anatomy. But in this group the assemblage of hip and pelvic bones more nearly resembles those of birds than of lizards. Consequently, the group's name is made up from the Greek words *ornithos,* meaning bird, and *ischios,* combined to translate freely as "bird-hipped."

The Saurischian pubis is in front and the ischium faces backward. But in the Ornithischian hip the pubis is parallel to the ischium, and in some types the pubis and ischium are fused. A fourth element exists in the latter type of pelvis. It is a forward-projecting bony process, extending out from the base of the pubis. This adds support to the Ornithischian belly region. Again, it is an advantage to animals that stand erect and move on two feet.

THE DINOSAUR PELVIC STRUCTURES

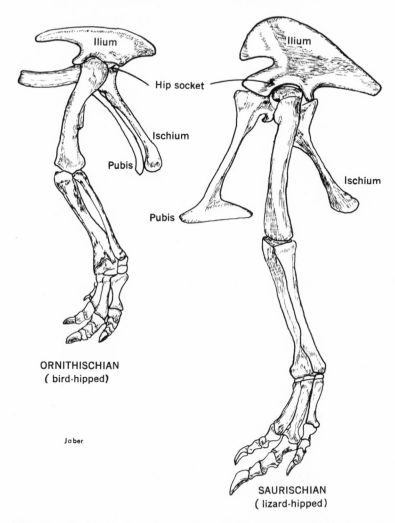

Ilium

Hip socket

Ischium

Pubis

Ilium

Ischium

Pubis

ORNITHISCHIAN
(bird-hipped)

Jaber

SAURISCHIAN
(lizard-hipped)

Fig. 9. The presence of a pelvic structure resembling that of birds should not be interpreted as an evolutionary relationship to birds. Actually, bird ancestry lies within the Saurischian line of descent.

The terms "bird-hipped" and "lizard-hipped" should not be taken to imply any evolutionary relationship with birds or lizards other than those of common ancestry.

There are more than 3,000 kinds of dinosaurs. Therefore, in a book of this size any attempt to take note of all of them would be a hopeless task. However, the major groups are distinguishable through representative types, and if we pick and choose carefully, all the basic evolutionary lines can be covered. Fortunately, there are hundreds of dinosaur types within some groups which share many features common to the group in which they belong and no other. There are, to be sure, a few types in which classification is difficult, but these problems need not concern the beginning student.

The plan adopted in this book is to take up the description of Saurischians and consider each of the suborders in turn, and then move on to the Ornithischians and do the same. The biggest difficulty with this plan is keeping the reader informed of the time relationships. Many dinosaurs in each of the suborders are not contemporaries at all, and spans of millions of years may separate some of the individual groups within each suborder.

For example, it is important to note that even though an animal is described as an ancestral form, the particular animal may persist relatively unchanged for millions of years, and thus may well be found as a contemporary among its remote descendants. The *Coelurosaurs* (SEE-loo-roh-sawrs), whom we shall meet as ancestors of the Saurischian order, are a good example. They persisted for millions of years in one form or another and kept on giving rise to many different groups, most of which existed side by side with the earlier forms, such as the particular one known as *Coelophysis* (see-loh-FAHY-sis). Coelurosaur is a name to remember—it will crop up very often in any outline or survey of the evolution of dinosaurs.

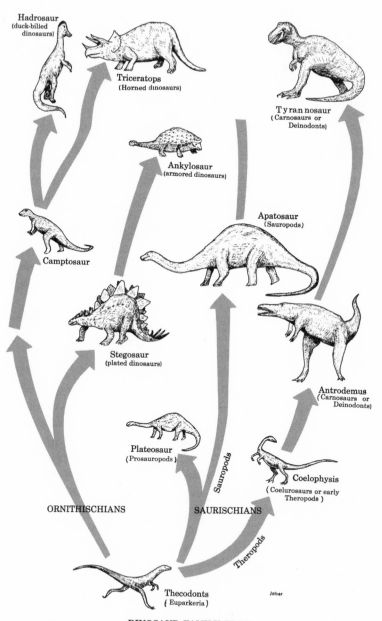

Hadrosaur
(duck-billed
dinosaurs)

Triceratops
(Horned dinosaurs)

Tyrannosaur
(Carnosaurs or
Deinodonts)

Ankylosaur
(armored dinosaurs)

Apatosaur
(Sauropods)

Camptosaur

Stegosaur
(plated dinosaurs)

Antrodemus
(Carnosaurs or
Deinodonts)

Plateosaur
(Prosauropods)

Coelophysis
(Coelurosaurs or early
Theropods)

ORNITHISCHIANS

SAURISCHIANS

Sauropods

Theropods

Thecodonts
(Euparkeria)

Jaber

DINOSAUR FAMILY TREE

The next two chapters cover the evolutionary lines of the two major orders. As an aid to understanding the two main lines of descent from the early Thecodonts, a dinosaur family tree has been provided here. This shows where the main groups fit in relation to each other and in time. It would be well to keep this family tree in mind while reading the two chapters.

CHAPTER 9

Saurischian Dinosaurs

This is the oldest branch and contains all the largest forms. It also comprises most of the carnivorous dinosaurs, which are members of one suborder called *Theropoda.* The one other suborder, the *Sauropoda,* is mainly an herbivorous group.

Saurischians derive directly from Thecodonts early in the Triassic period. The most primitive types were small, swift, bipedal, carnivorous animals, represented by *Euparkeria* (you-par-KEHR-ee-uh). It was the first animal to walk erect on two legs. Its immediate descendant is the swifter and more streamlined Coelophysis.

Coelophysis was about eight or ten feet long when fully grown. Despite its comparatively large size, it probably weighed less than fifty pounds. The bones of Coelophysis were graceful and lightly constructed. This animal was obviously built for speed. The skull was hinged loosely at the end of a long neck, and its jaws held sharp serrated teeth.

Coelophysis may also have been cannibalistic. Skeletons of other, smaller Coelophysis dinosaurs were found inside one adult skeleton. But speculations are that these might represent embryonic forms or stages, and it could be that

Euparkeria
(Thecodont)

Length: 3 ft.

Jaber

Fig. 11. A Triassic period thecodont, the ancestor of all dino-saurs, birds, crocodiles, and the flying reptiles. Its immediate descendants were the small, agile, and fierce predators, the coelurosaurs, which are the first dinosaurs. See Fig. 12.

Coelophysis gave birth to live young—a very unreptilelike birth method (though it is not unknown in modern reptiles).

The animals derived from Coelophysis are known as *Coelurosaurs*. They evolved into many different forms, but mainly along two evolutionary paths: toward the first plant-eating dinosaurs (herbivores) and toward carnivorous preda-tors. However, the predacious (predator) group also branched out in two directions. They began to evolve giant types of dinosaurs on the one hand, and small, swift, elegant bipedal predacious forms on the other. These latter were not too different from the original Coelophysis ancestor.

A large number of reptile groups were in existence by the end of the Triassic period. They had become adapted to many kinds of environments. There were large and small predators, giant carnivorous crocodilelike swamp dwellers

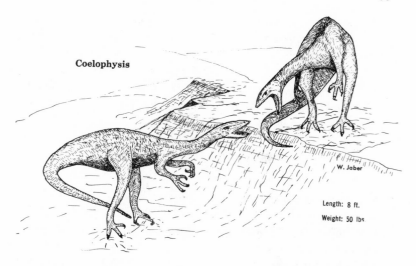

Coelophysis

Length: 8 ft.
Weight: 50 lbs

W. Jaber

Fig. 12. The ancestor of all carnivorous dinosaurs was small, agile, very light in weight, very fast and ferocious. Coelophysis may also have been cannibalistic. This belief derives from the discovery of small Coelophysis skeletons inside larger specimens of the same species. However, some say this is merely an indication that the young were born live, and not from layed eggs, the usual method of birth in dinosaurs.

(the ferocious *Phytosaurs* (FAHY-toh-sawrs), armored Thecodont reptiles, turtles, lizards, and the declining mammallike reptiles (*Pelycosaurs*).

But in all the hundreds of groups and kinds of animals on land, there were no herbivores until the Saurischians evolved them. Even the lowly labyrinthodont amphibians, which by now were moving toward extinction, were mostly carnivorous.

There had been a predator-prey relationship among animals long before the development of plant eaters. It consisted of larger animals devouring smaller ones. Food nutrients and energy passed from the very small animals up to the largest in this predator-prey relationship. But when plant eaters were introduced to the world, an enormous reservoir of new food nutrients for the production of energy was released to the world's ecological system. When the Coelurosaurs evolved a tribe of herbivores, they removed the last barriers to the dinosaur conquest of the earth.

The rise of plant-eating animals changed the character of the predator-prey relationship. Animals that thrived on vegetation began to far out number carnivorous animals that preyed on them. There developed a ratio of vegetarians to meat eaters. The dinosaurs exploited new environments and then began rapidly to expand in both numbers and kinds of animals. Many of the new types were largely vegetarians. As the latter got larger, there developed even larger predators to prey on them. Hence, the tendency toward giantism proceeded in both carnivores and herbivores.

The development of herbivorous dinosaur groups took place near the end of the Triassic period. It is no surprise that it is at this time that the dinosaurs finally took over the world. They quickly radiated outward into all the remaining land environments and literally overshadowed their contemporary reptile cousins and overwhelmed the already declining amphibian ancestor groups. The mammallike reptiles disappeared altogether; the amphibians persisted only in very small types. The mammals were completely outclassed and continued to be insignificant figures in a landscape that belonged to the ruling reptiles—the dinosaurs. Thus, the Age of Reptiles, which began in the Permian period, expanded at the end of the Triassic period to become the Age of Dinosaurs.

However, at the time the herbivorous dinosaurs began to evolve, there was only one order of dinosaurs, the Saurischians. The herbivores developed within the Saurischian

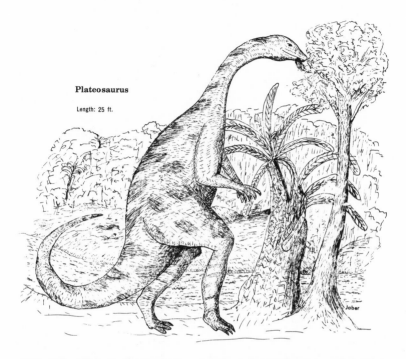

Plateosaurus

Length: 25 ft.

Fig. 13. This is the largest animal of the Triassic period. It is the immediate ancestor of the giant herbivorous four-footed sauropod dinosaurs. But Plateosaurus was bipedal, although it may have occasionally gotten down on all fours.

order. Their actual ancestor was a Coelurosaurian group known as the *Prosauropoda*. They are considered the intermediate form that later gave rise to the true herbivorous types. They were not entirely herbivorous, however. They were no larger than Coelophysis, their ancestor, which was seven or eight feet long.

SUBORDER SAUROPODA. The Prosauropod dinosaurs, best represented by *Platersaurus* (see fig. 13.), became the giants of their day, but they were a far cry from the size of their descendants, the Sauropods, in the next period (Jurassic).

The Jurassic herbivorous dinosaurs developed massive bodies, heavy, pillarlike legs, long necks and tails, and very small heads. The largest animal that ever lived on land is a Sauropod dinosaur. They represent the popular conception of dinosaurs, when it is not distorted by the motion-picture version. The children's conception (see the Introduction) is the truest form, but many versions of it are misleading because they contain erroneous details.

The Sauropod is the most astonishing animal that ever lived. Nearly everything about it bears the stamp of improbability. There are numerous questions about it that have no adequate answers. For example, it is known that the teeth were not very well developed and the head was certainly very small. Since the dinosaur weighed as much as seventy tons, how is it possible that such a hulking body could be maintained in its food requirements by means of the puny mouth and teeth? It is known that it was partially aquatic, a dweller in swamps or shallow basins, and probably subsisted mainly on a diet of soft marsh vegetation.

The principal Sauropods include *Apatosaurus* (a-PAT-oh-sawr-us), formerly known as *Brontosaurus, Diplodocus* (dahy-PLOH-doh-kus), the model for many fictional and children's versions, and *Brachiosaurus* (brack-ee-oh-SAWR-us), the largest land animal that ever lived. The latter animal reached a length of seventy-five feet (twenty-three meters); it was forty feet (fifteen meters) high, and it weighed up to seventy tons, exceeded in animals only by the modern blue whale.

Because of their great weight, most scientists assume that they were partially aquatic, but there are authorities who dispute this. For example, Robert Bakker has reconstructed

TWO SAUROPOD DINOSAURS

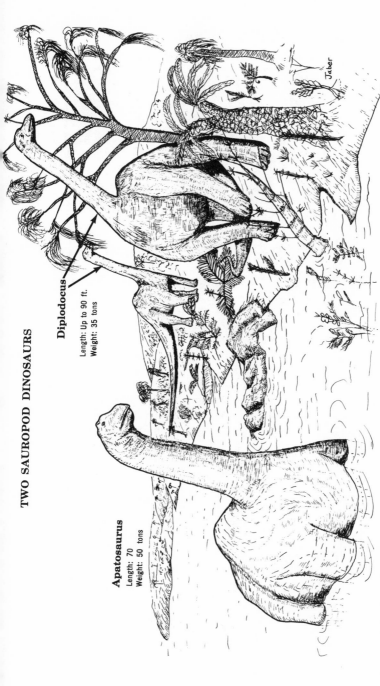

Diplodocus

Length: Up to 90 ft.
Weight: 35 tons

Apatosaurus

Length: 70
Weight: 50 tons

Fig. 14. Although Apatosaurus is still regarded as having been a dweller in swamps, marshes, and shorelines, Diplodocus is now thought by many paleontologists to have been mostly a land dweller. Herds of Diplodocus may have roamed through Jurassic forests.

Brachiosaurus
Length: 80 ft.
Weight: 60 tons
Height: 40 ft.

William Jaber

Fig. 15.   The heaviest land animal that ever lived, it was unusual in shape for a sauropod—its front legs were longer in shape than the hind legs. Brachiosaurus could have looked over a three-story building. The presence of a nasal opening high up on the head reveals that it was a browser in swamp forests and was partially aquatic in habits.

certain Sauropods with giraffelike necks and claims they were tree browsers. There are also a number of reputable claims that Sauropods roamed in herds, moving through Jurassic forests in much the same way as present-day elephants.

The Sauropods were common in Africa, Europe, Asia, and in both Americas. They became extinct in northern North America before the end of the Age of Dinosaurs. Their only natural enemy was probably the great *Theropod Carnosaurs* which we will meet up with next.

SUBORDER THEROPODA. The other major subdivision of the Saurischians is the Theropod suborder. It evolved from the Coelurosaurs and branched out in the Jurassic period to form two groups. One of these was the *Deinodonts* (DEH-noh-donts), "terror teeth," which includes the largest meat-eating animals that ever lived. The Deinodonts were ponderous, bipedal (two-footed), ferocious predators and voracious hunters. They were the most feared of all dinosaurs.

Antrodemus (an-TROH-dee-mus), also known as *Allosaur*, was an early Jurassic form, and probably ancestral to the two later (and larger) Theropods. All three were nature's greatest

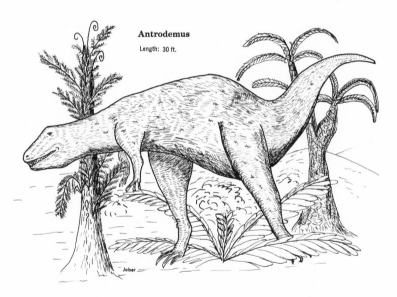

Antrodemus
Length: 30 ft.

Fig. 16. Formerly known as Allosaurus, meaning "jumping lizard," Antrodemus was no lizard. It was the largest meat-eating animal of its time—the Jurassic period. The cycad-like tree and the fern tree were common Jurassic plants.

killing machines. Antrodemus measured up to 34 feet (10.5 meters) in length and weighed up to four tons. Its old name, Allosaur, means "jumping lizard," apparently because its hind legs appear to have been highly developed, both for speed as well as for a jumping ability.

Later, in the *Cretaceous* period (the third and last period of the Mesozoic era), *Gorgosaurus* appeared. This was a thirty-five-foot North American predator. But the culminating form of Deinodont, and the last to evolve, was *Tyrannosaurus rex*. It had a head up to 4 feet long, and it was a full 19 feet (5.8 meters) above the ground. In its jaws were two

Tyrannosaurus rex
Length: 50 ft.
Weight 10 tons
Height: 16 ft.

William Jaber

Fig. 17. This is the largest meat-eating land animal that ever lived and was the largest theropod dinosaur. Some authorities state flatly that Tyrannosaurus rex was the most powerful animal that ever evolved in the earth's history.

rows of 6-inch, daggerlike teeth. This dinosaur attained a length of up to 47 feet (14.2 meters) and stood on two huge trunklike legs, using its ponderous tail as a balance. Its two front feet were ridiculously small appendages, which probably served only to help to prop the animal when it began to rise up off the ground from its prone resting position. Tyrannosaurus rex came at the very end of the Age of Dinosaurs and represents the highest development of the Theropod form.

One very strange Theropod dinosaur from Colorado was *Ceratosaurus* (seh-RAT-oh-sawr-us). It was very similar in

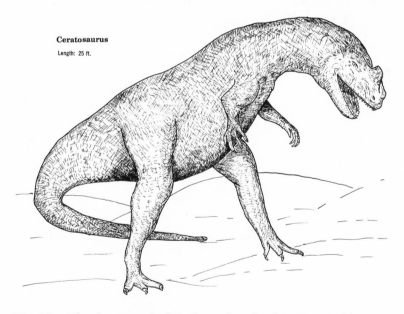

Ceratosaurus
Length: 25 ft.

Fig. 18. This ferocious-looking beast has the distinction of being the only horned carnosaur (meat-eating dinosaur). It very closely resembles Antrodemus (see Fig. 16), and some scientists say it is the same animal. They claim that the horn may be an abnormal growth, peculiar to this one particular specimen.

most respects to Antrodemus. Both were about thirty feet long. They were swift, well-balanced, bipedal predators. But Ceratosaurus had something extra—a horn on its nose. It is the only known Carnosaur with a horn.

Later Coelurosaurs. The Coelurosaurs were the ancestors not only of the great Theropod Deinodonts and the Sauropods, but they gave rise to a number of other groups of dinosaurs in astonishing variety. Most were small, bipedal, swift runners, and all were carnivorous. They had enormously improved balancing and speed abilities. Nearly all of them were streamlined and more birdlike. Some were no bigger than chickens.

One of them—*Compsognathus* (comp-sog-NATH-us)—is the smallest dinosaur known. It was the size of a small chicken.

Another type of Coelurosaur is the "ostrich dinosaur." Its

Compsognathus

Length: 2 ft.

Jaber

Fig. 19. The smallest known dinosaur. It was no bigger than a chicken, and it may have been cannibalistic, feeding upon the young of its own species.

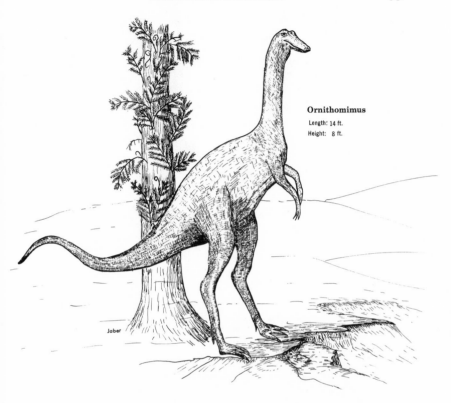

Ornithomimus
Length: 14 ft.
Height: 8 ft.

Jaber

Fig. 20. This is one of several types of "ostrich dinosaurs." It is an excellent example of evolutionary convergence—animals that evolved similar forms but are not related. This Saurischian dinosaur is totally unrelated to birds. It lived in North America and Asia. The tree is an extinct Mesozoic age fern tree.

scientific name is *Ornithomimus* (or-nee-thoh-MEE-mus), meaning "bird imitator." This dinosaur is essentially an advanced model of the old Coelophysis. It is almost as if nature was experimenting, which it is, in reality. Ornithomimus had grasping hands, a long neck, and in other respects resembled the modern ostrich (which did not exist at that time). Or-

Fig. 21. This is the principal member of a group of small but ferocious predators, known as dromeosaurs. The sharp oversize claw, the animal's obvious speed and balancing abilities, and its rigid straight tail, all indicate that Deinonychus was a highly specialized dinosaur—a refined killing machine—and very likely it was warm-blooded like the modern mammals.

nithomimus may have been a fruit picker, too, but it was essentially a Carnosaur, even though it had no teeth. This strange animal also had a beaklike jaw. This feature, combined with the fact that it had no teeth, makes one wonder about the closeness and the parallelism that keeps cropping up between dinosaurs and birds.

One final interesting fact about Ornithomimus is that it may have been a stealer of eggs. One skeleton was found in Mongolia in the company of eggs from a different kind of dinosaur. That Ornithomimid has been named *Oviraptor* (oh-vee-RAP-ter), or the "egg stealer."

One of the swiftest, and probably the most ferocious of the small Theropod dinosaurs, was *Deinonychus* (dahy-non-EE-kus), or "terrible claw." This animal had a prominent forward-pointing claw on each of its two hind feet. These claws were undoubtedly offensive weapons. Deinonychus seemed to have such good balance in its proportions that it very likely could have stood on one leg and used its claw to disembowel its prey. (See page 96). It was about eight feet long. Deinonychus lived in what is now Montana and Wyoming early in the *Cretaceous* period, the last period of the Mesozoic.

CHAPTER 10

Ornithischian Dinosaurs

The bird-hipped dinosaurs did not appear until the Sauris-chians were well along in the development of giant preda-tors. Consequently, Ornithischians were surrounded by a host of meat-eating dinosaurs. Carnosaurs undoubtedly dined often at the expense of great herds or populations of Ornithis-chians.

Although Ornithischians evolved from Thecodont ances-tors, and thus do share a very distant kinship to the Sauris-chians, there is no Triassic fossil record to speak of. They are essentially Jurassic-Cretaceous dinosaurs. Since we don't know what the earliest ones looked like, scientists have searched among the later dinosaurs for archaic forms that might serve as a model on which to reconstruct as far as possible the ancestral Ornithischians. About all they could surmise with any accuracy, without a model, is that the first Ornithischians were bipedal and probably quite small.

Fortunately, there was a later dinosaur that represents an ancient dynasty which probably evolved very slowly and perhaps carries many of the features of the early Ornithis-chians. This is the Cretaceous dinosaur *Hypsilophodon* (hip-sih-LOH-foh-don). It was a bipedal animal with strong hind

Hypsilophodon
Length: 5 ft.

Drawn by Jaber

Fig. 22.   Although it is a late dinosaur—of Cretaceous age—Hypsilophodon has certain basic primitive features in its anatomy, and thus is used as a model for reconstructing the earliest Ornithischians, of which none are known. Hypsilophodon is thought to have been a tree climber. Its direct ancestors appear to have been the thecodonts.

limbs, small forelimbs, and a long tail. Hypsilophodon had a birdlike pelvis, but it was not nearly as birdlike as the typical Ornithischian of late Jurassic and Cretaceous time. It may have walked on all fours at times, or during particular stages of growth, and there is good indication that it was a tree climber—judged mostly from the fact that its toes were developed for grasping.

Thus, with Hypsilophodon as a model, researchers decided that the earliest known Ornithischian dinosaur was *Camptosaurus*. All Ornithischians that were bipedal have been classified in the suborder *Ornithopoda*. This usually includes *Camptosaurus*, the Iguanodons (ih-GWAH-noh-dons), the dome-headed dinosaurs, and the Hadrosaurs, all of which

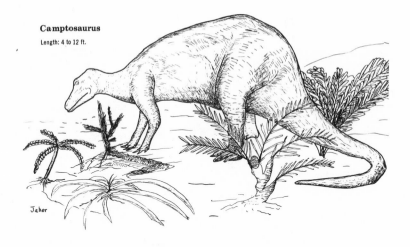

Camptosaurus
Length: 4 to 12 ft.

Fig. 23. This early North American Ornithischian probably walked on all four feet at least some of the time. However, it is the principal ancestor of the great bipedal Ornithischians, such as Trachodon and the hadrosaurs.

will be described below. The other major groups are the plated dinosaurs, the horned dinosaurs, and the armored dinosaurs. Thus, the Camptosaurs are sometimes regarded as a suborder. If so, then there are seven major groups of Ornithischians.

The Iguanodon is a large, bipedal dinosaur about thirty feet long, with fairly large forelimbs. One peculiar feature of the animal was the presence of a spikelike thumb. The use for this appendage is unknown. Otherwise, Iguanodons resemble the earlier Camptosaurs.

The Iguanodons were the first dinosaurs to be discovered by human beings. It was an Iguanodon's tooth that the Eng-

Iguanodon
Length. 30 ft.
Weight: 7 tons
Height: 16 ft.

Fig. 24. A big dinosaur in a running pose—an obvious clue that old concepts of dinosaurs are changing. It is now supposed that the large bipedal animals such as Iguanodon used their heavy tails as balances, so they could lean forward in a loping gait. Such a habit would require a lot more energy than the traditional concept of dinosaurs allows. There are still many scientists who deny that dinosaurs ever had this high energy use type of locomotion.

lish paleontologist, Gideon Mantell, discovered in 1822 (see Chapter 2). Actually, the real discoverer was his wife, but history gave him the credit. Cuvier had at first identified this tooth as being from a rhinoceros. The largest, most complete, and most valuable dinosaur fossil discovery ever made was that of a large group of Iguanodons found in 1877, one thousand feet underground in a coal mine at Bernissart, Belgium. In this connection, there is one more very important person who should be identified. He is Louis Dollo (1858–1931), a French paleontologist who spent his entire professional career on one single project: the restoration and study of the Bernissart Iguanodons. Dollo restored thirty-one complete skeletons.

Apparently the animals had fallen into a ravine and were quickly covered by debris and sediments laid down by running water over 130 million years ago.

The *Pachycephalosaurus* (pack-ee-CEF-uh-loh-sawr-us), or dome-headed dinosaur, is of the late Cretaceous period. It was one of the last dinosaurs to appear and is one of the strangest looking animals, too. The skull was a solid dome, studded with knobs and small spikes all around and on the nose.

Hadrosaur is the name given to the large group of duck-billed dinosaurs, also of late Cretaceous time. They are somewhat related to the dome-headed dinosaurs and to the Iguanodons. The Hadrosaurs, or "duck-billed" dinosaurs, get their name from the flat, broad appearance of the nose and bill—it looks like the bill of a duck. Each side of the jaw had over 500 teeth. They are a great mystery, principally because they developed so many different kinds of head styles. The many kinds of duck-billed dinosaurs all had similar bodies. But the heads presented a great variety in forms and anatomical mysteries. Most of these animals were quite large—

up to about 40 feet long. All were herbivorous, and until recently, it was assumed that all duck-billed dinosaurs were marsh or swamp dwellers. But there is some evidence to dispute that now. It is not a certainty either way. There may have been both "upland" and "lowland" types of Hadrosaurs, each group adapted to its particular environment. Moreover, there may have been stages of growth in which these animals lived away from water.

There were three types of Hadrosaurs (duck-billed dinosaurs): the flat-headed type, represented by *Trachodon*, the solid-crested, represented by *Saurolophus* (sawr-oh-LOH-fus), and hollow-crested, with *Corythosaurus* (koh-ree-thoh-SAWR-us) as a typical example.

The crested dinosaurs came in many varieties. The solid-crested types, such as Saurolophus, were really a flat-headed form with one bone enlarged into a crest on top of the skull. However, the crest was not hollow. It was formed in Saurolo-

Corythosaurus
Length: 25 ft.

William Jaber

Fig. 25.   This is one of several types of hollow-crested madrosaurs. Its premaxillary bones (a pair of bones in the upper jaw) and its nasal bone are greatly expanded to form a hollow cap-like crest that covers the top of the skull. No one is sure what the purpose was of this evolutionary detail in the skull.

phus by an enlargement of the nasal bone. It did not serve as a horn. In fact, the crest's purpose is unknown. Some authorities claim that skin covered the crest.

The hollow-crested dinosaur has a nasal passage that winds up through the crest bone and then back down to the throat. Again there appears to be no real purpose for this, but studies on these animals are still in progress, and there may someday be an answer to the crest question. Some of the crests, like that of the Corythosaurus in Figure 25, look like a helmet, while that of *Parasaurolophus* looks like one backward sweeping horn of a goat that has lost its other horn. Some say that these types contain air chambers as reservoirs of extra air for use while the animal's head is under water; others say that the hollow-crested Hadosaur used the passageway to sharpen its sense of smell.

Certainly the Hadrosaurs appear to have had very keen eyesight and very good hearing organs. They also seem to have been equipped to make vocal sounds. Evidence indicates that Hadrosaurs were very alert. Many of them were probably aquatic, and certainly they were sensitive and very successful. They represent the highest form of dinosaur.

The largest of all Hadrosaurs is *Trachodon*, also known as Anatosaurus. It was forty feet long and weighed several tons. It had massive, heavy legs, and walked erect, like all the Hadrosaurs. It probably was web-rooted. Its tail anatomy, like that of most Hadrosaurs, shows that it was probably a good swimmer.

PLATED DINOSAURS. These are among the oldest dinosaurs, and for most purposes we need to discuss only the one genus—*Stegosauria.* The Stegosaurs arose early in the Jurassic period and died out completely before the end of the Age of Dinosaurs. In other words, they were the first major group to become extinct.

The Stegosaur was four-footed, about twenty feet long

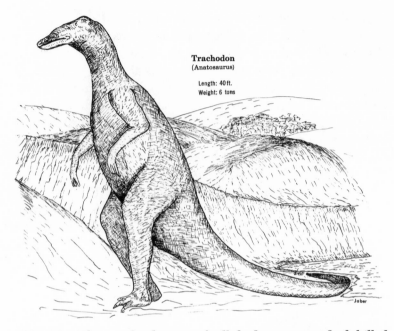

Fig. 26. This is the largest of all hadrosaurs or duck-billed dinosaurs. It had webbed hands but no web between the toes. Trachodon lived in North America in late Cretaceous time.

when full-grown, and it stood eight feet high at the hips. The skeleton forms an arc with its high point over the pelvis, and the animal is known for its tiny head, almost ridiculously small. Its brain was about the size of a walnut and probably did little more than supervise the action of the jaws. It had about twenty-five small weak teeth.

It is known as a plated dinosaur because of its armor, which consisted of a double row of triangular long plates right down the middle of the back. These end at the tail, which was armed with spikes on the end. The plates were vertical, but their exact positioning on the back is a matter of dispute between paleontologists. More important, however, are the theories about the function of these plates.

Stegosaurus
Length: 25 ft.
Height: 8 ft. at the hips
Weight: 4 tons

Fig. 27. Stegosaurs are puzzling and strange to the scientists. Their bizarre appearance is heightened by the tiny head, with a brain the size of a walnut. The spinal plates are an outlandish burden. Stegosaurs also had an enlarged "solar plexus" (a spinal nerve in the pelvic region), which some say acted as a second brain.

They don't seem to be very effective armor, but some experts believe their presence was meant less as armor than as a device to frighten the enemy.

Stegosaurs have been found in North America, Europe, and Africa, but it is fairly certain that they were almost world-wide in distribution. No one really knows why they became extinct so early.

Some popular literature depicts Stegosaurs being eaten by the giant Tyrannosaurs. But this is a misconception, since they were not contemporaries. The Stegosaurs died out before Tyrannosaurs developed.

ARMORED DINOSAURS. Better known as *Ankylosaurs* (AN-kee-loh-saurs), meaning "crooked lizard," the armored dinosaurs arose just as the Stegosaurs were disappearing. In fact, the two groups are related in several ways. Anatomically there are striking similarities between Stegosaurs and Ankylosaurs, despite the differences in their outward appearances. The position, carriage, and size of the head, the shape and form of the forelimbs, and the broad feet all reveal that both the plated dinosaurs and the armored dinosaurs had bipedal, perhaps common ancestors.

Ankylosaurs had small teeth and lived on soft vegetation. One group, called *Nodosaur*, meaning "toothless lizard," did not have teeth. Their armor covered the whole body, and in some types there were rows of big heavy spines or horned protuberances, while other parts of the body were protected by heavy, flat, bone covering. Some of them had plates of bone all the way down the tail. They had spiked tails. Their armor was quite effective against animals such as the Gorgosaurs and Tyrannosaurs—their predator contemporaries. The Ankylosaurs were very successful animals and survived right up to the end of the Age of Dinosaurs. Whatever killed them off, killed off all dinosaurs, so they were no less fit than any other.

It should be noted also that Ankylosaurs had traits not unlike the modern armadillos, although they are in no way related, not even remotely. The best-known Ankylosaur is *Polacanthus,* a European variety with a double row of spikes along the back and protected elsewhere on its body by long plates, a kind of bone mail, made up of a mosaic of tiny bones. Ankylosaurs reached a length of about 25 feet (7.5 meters) and weighed up to 4 tons.

HORNED DINOSAURS.   They are known in science as the *Ceratopsians.* They evolved from an animal called *Psittacosaurus* (sit-tuh-KOH-sawr-us), which means "parrot beak." That is one trait all the Ceratopsians have. The front part of the skull above the mouth is bent over in the manner of a

Fig. 28. Armored dinosaurs appeared just at the time when plated dinosaurs (the stegosaurs) were being extinct. Ankylosaurs filled the environments left vacant by the dying stegosaurs.

parrot's beak. But a more direct ancestor of Ceratopsians may be the *Leptoceratops,* a six-foot dinosaur of Alberta, Canada. This is the animal from which evolved the first true Ceratopsians—*Protoceratops.* Protoceratops fossils were first discovered in Mongolia. The animal weighed about 900 pounds and was up to seven feet long.

Giantism developed rather quickly among the Ceratopsians, presumably because the predators, such as the Gorgosaurs and Tyrannosaurs, were giants. *Monoclonius,* a fifteen-foot Ceratopsian from Alberta, Canada, was the first of a number of giant forms. Monoclonius had a long nasal horn, somewhat like that of a rhinoceros.

The last and greatest of all Ceratopsians was *Triceratops* (trahy-SER-uh-tops), a twenty-foot, heavily armored, three-horned beast that weighed up to eight tons. This animal is often pictured in mortal combat with Tyrannosaurus rex. The truth is that it was more than a match for that ferocious hunter, and probably won more battles with Tyrannosaurus

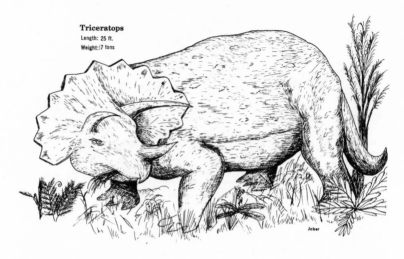

Fig. 29. There were many kinds of horned dinosaurs. This was one of the largest and was the last to evolve. It was a North American animal that roamed in large herds in Wyoming, Montana, and the Alberta province of western Canada.

than it lost. If such is true, Triceratops, a vegetarian, might well qualify as the mightiest land animal that ever lived. Whatever its rank in our imagination, it certainly does qualify as nature's supreme contribution in armored tanks!

Ceratopsians were active browsers and probably traveled in groups. They must have presented an awesome sight roaming through the uplands of prehistoric western North America and eastern Asia. Apparently marine or mountain barriers prevented their passage into other parts of the world.

It is fitting that any history of the dinosaurs should end with Triceratops and its breed, for they were the very last dinosaurs to die out in the great crisis—whatever that may have been—that ended the Mesozoic era and destroyed the great dinosaur family. They were huge, and strangely beautiful animals, developed to the highest degree possible for defense purposes. If these peaceful grazers had not been among the last great tribes of dinosaurs, it would have been easier to consign the dinosaurs to nature's trash heap as failures. But the Ceratopsians, above all, were not failures. They survived for perhaps 50 million years in a world that was obviously becoming an impossible place for dinosaurs, all dinosaurs.

But they had no brain to speak of—they could not invent a spaceship and escape their fate—there was no way out for them.

CHAPTER 11

Extinction

Mass death had overtaken living things in previous geologic periods. But whatever occurred at the end of the Cretaceous period was so devastating that it not only ended the period, but the Mesozoic era as well. The most important fact about this event, or series of events, was that at the close of Cretaceous history, the reptiles were dethroned from their position of leadership. This was accomplished when they vacated the main ecological niches of the world's environments. That is to say, the large grazing reptiles, the big predators that stalked the browsers and grazers, the large swamp dwellers, the agile, speedy forest dinosaurs, the flying reptiles, and the large marine reptiles, all vacated their ranges and were replaced by animals of a different class—usually either birds or mammals. The Age of Reptiles and also the Age of Dinosaurs came to an end.

It should be emphasized, however, that this did not all happen overnight. It took several million years. It was a holocaust only in the geologic sense, when looked at in relation to the vast span of time encompassed by the total history of life. The slowness in human terms must be kept in mind, because with this concept we can perceive that some events in the great crisis probably happened as a result of others. There might have been a domino effect to some extent— some extinctions were caused by others, and that much of the crisis may have been triggered by a series of events, or changes that ran in sequence. Before we investigate the cause or causes, let us first be certain of what really happened. The following are the major events:

1. Flowering plants, which first appeared in Jurassic time, finally became worldwide in distribution.
2. The modern fishes exploded into a rapid radiation, pushing out some older types of marine life.
3. All the marine reptiles, except turtles, disappeared.
4. The flying reptiles became extinct and were replaced by the toothless birds.
5. The toothed birds disappeared.
6. The ruling reptile groups on land became extinct, leaving four orders of smaller reptiles—snakes, lizards, crocodiles, and turtles. That means that at least ten groups of reptiles became extinct.
7. The Atlantic Ocean began to form; Continental Drift was proceeding.
8. Shallow seas invaded continental margins at least twice during the Cretaceous period, but on the last invasion, much of Europe and North America were inundated.
9. A dramatic dying out occurred among many kinds of Cephalopod mollusks and other shelled animals, obviously as a result of drastic changes in several marine environments— changes in sea depth, shorelines, temperatures, etc.
10. Climates greatly altered in many places, and there is some evidence both for glaciers and deserts at various times during the 75 million years of the Cretaceous period. There may have been an Ice Age of several million years extent, especially in the former Gondwanaland (southern continent).
11. Mammals and toothless birds radiated quickly to fill up the vacant niches left by the extinct reptiles.

It is interesting to note that some dinosaurs anticipated the great destruction that finally overwhelmed the Mesozoic world, and they became extinct before the others. These were the Stegosaurs (plated dinosaurs). A record of the declining populations of the later dinosaurs has been preserved in two formations of rocks: the Belly River stage and the Lance stage, located in Montana and the southern Alberta province of western Canada. An investigation of these stages show that in every instance where a count of fossils was obtained, the Lance stage (the last rocks of Cretaceous age) always had a lower count than the Belly River rocks, the next layer down, and slightly older—farther back in the Cretaceous period. For example, in the Belly River stage sixteen horned dinosaurs (Ceratopsians) were discovered to only seven in the Lance.

The famous Hadrosaurs (duck-billed dinosaurs) dropped from twenty-nine in Belly River to only seven in the Lance. These figures show the quite remarkable dropping off of populations of dinosaurs. The various types of dinosaurs began to drop out altogether as the top layers of Cretaceous rocks are reached. The Ceratopsian or horned dinosaurs are the very last to be recorded. In the top layer of the Lance stage rocks of Montana, there were still numerous Ceratopsians, proving that these animals—they were peaceful grazers—hung on to the very end. And then right above that, they are gone forever. One wonders what happened to this dinosaur's natural enemy, the great Theropod predator *Tyrannosaurus rex*. Why is this dinosaur not found in the same rocks? It would be a great irony for the Ceratopsians to have outlived their natural enemy, only to succumb to some other disaster. This is probably what did happen.

CHAPTER 12

Whatever Happened to the Dinosaurs?

Most paleontologists now believe that the extinctions were the result of a whole series of events that were taking place simultaneously or in rapid sequence throughout most of the Cretaceous period. Only a decade ago, however, a book such as this one would have been appended at the end with a long list of possible reasons for the Mesozoic disaster. There is no need to do that now, for one of the benefits of modern science has been to narrow down the number of possible causes.

In addition, the new sciences of paleomagnetism, Continental Drift (plate tectonics), paleoecology, and paleoclimatology have restructured what we know about the 75-million-year Cretaceous period. This has provided one additional good cause for the extinctions, amid a number of still acceptable theories that are listed in older textbooks. Among some discarded theories are speculations about the deleterious effects of the flowering plants on dinosaurs. There were theories of poisoning, tooth abrasion through plant foraging, constipation, and the displacement of animals through the influences of migrating plants, principally the theory that migrating, nonedible plants overwhelmed dinosaur grazing lands, and so forth.

With our present knowledge of climate changes that were possible and probable as the natural effects of Continental Drift, we can now, with some assurance, place some of the blame for the disappearance of dinosaurs on changing climates. But the alteration of climate is not the whole story. Continental Drift had other consequences aside from causing radical long-term changes in climates.

Some consequences of Continental Drift include:

the establishing of oceanic climates (cool, moist climates—Köppen's *Cfb,* and *Df* climates) on several continents where they had not been before; the movement away from the equatorial belt by much of the continental land masses; the alternate inundation and then draining of continental shelf land when ocean floors deepened (a process that seems to have accelerated in the Cretaceous period); the poleward movement of much habitable land, causing an excessive cooling trend compared to the earlier widespread subtropical climates that dinosaurs flourished under; the creation of rain barriers through the elevating of much land as the result of collisions between plate blocks (see Chapter 6); the spreading of desert climates by virtue of the increase in rain-shadow highlands, and because of changes in the jet stream configuration; the radiation outward of plants and animals favored by the new climates, in opposition to plants and animals that previously enjoyed, and were adapted to, warmer climates; the extreme reduction in subtropical marshlands, favored especially by the Sauropods and Hadrosaurs; the elevation of highlands through increased volcanism, continental rifting, and continental collision.

All these and more contributed to altering environments for dinosaurs. The larger forms would be the natural targets of most of the changes. Even the elimination of Ichthyosaurs and Plesiosaurs can be explained by dint of a myriad of changes in the water environments that resulted from the breakup of Pangaea. (Recent sensational evidence was offered to prove the continued existence of the giant marine reptile *Plesiosaurus,* which is not a dinosaur. But again, the purveyors of the evidence—Japanese fishermen—failed to present convincing scientific proof. For one thing, they failed to retain the exhibit dredged up from the Pacific Ocean floor, and for another, it was poorly photographed.)

The breakup of Pangaea and its two major parts, Laurasia and Gondwanaland, had a lot to do with dinosaur extinctions. The breakup imposed a physical barrier which prevented the radiation of new groups to other continents. As a consequence, in some instances, instead of an adapted animal being able to enter a continent where it would flourish under new conditions, the physical barrier (an ocean or sea) isolated the breeding populations. In this way, adaptable genes in other parts of the world were not available for use on the continent where it might well have given the group a chance to evolve species that could survive the new conditions.

One example of widespread disruptions in life systems can be seen in the birds. Note that the birds and Pterosaurs (flying reptiles) probably ran head-on in competitive struggle. The victory of the birds and the extinction of Pterosaurs were inevitable if consideration is made of all changes that had a very high probability of occurring—displacement of nesting areas, nest robbery, egg stealing, niche deterioration through climatic change, radiation of new natural enemies, the development of superior flight mechanisms in birds, new plant species and their foragers, and, finally, wholesale radical changes in climate and the erection of solid mountain barriers to migration. Considering all these factors, the extinction of Pterosaurs is no mystery at all.

And the extinction of dinosaurs is less mysterious if some of the mystery is taken out of the science of ecology. Ecology is the science which treats all living things in their relationship to the environment. It is not difficult to see that every living thing on earth is intimately associated with every other living thing. What happens in one part of the world can have a domino effect on all the other plant and animal associations.

Ecology in the Mesozoic era was no different from today. In the Mesozoic, natural or extraterrestrial events interposed some ecologically destructive agent. The best guess today is that the agent which set loose the destructive storm of changes was Continental Drift, and the breakup of Pangaea.

Climatologists today are frantically searching for people willing to listen to their urgent warnings that our climatic systems are delicate mechanisms that can be altered with unknown and possibly terrifying consequences. Something like this probably did happen at the end of the Mesozoic, brought on by an accidental confluence of two or more natural events of worldwide scope and influence.

One of these events is almost certainly Continental Drift, probably accompanied by a very large increase in volcanic activity, orogeny (mountain building), and the swift, alternate displacement or redistribution of water and land.

Volcanic activity would have created a heat blanket possibly by an increase in CO_2 (carbon dioxide levels) and ash, which might have quickly led to what scientists call a "greenhouse" effect. This is the trapping of solar energy which has succeeded in reaching the earth but cannot be reflected back to outer space because it has become long-wavelength energy and is blocked by the dust particles and carbon dioxide. Thus, the earth took on a lower *albedo*—a lower ratio of reflected light to that received. This increased the heat retained. It could have led either to the melting of icecaps or to an ice age, depending on other factors.

The number of events, both physical and biological, which were the consequence of Continental Drift, and which are interrelated is staggering. If all these could be traced as to their total degree of interaction, it would be less of a mystery that dinosaurs failed to survive the end of the Mesozoic.

But the exact manner in which one set of factors influenced another, setting off a chain reaction of results ending in mass death, are unknown and probably never will be known.

The fact is that it is still correct to conjecture that there is more than one reason for the extinction of dinosaurs, but the reasons have changed from what we thought they were up to about 1960. The reasons are all interrelated ones—they are the dominoes of ecological disaster, triggered to fall by Continental Drift.

CHAPTER 13

Were They Really Reptiles?

As was noted earlier, at first paleontologists accepted Owen's decision to regard dinosaurs as reptiles, but not as lizards. No one today seriously entertains the idea that they were lizards, but there is growing uneasiness about the assumption that they were reptiles. Some scientists smoothed over their doubts by simply admitting that they could be reptiles, but if so, they were very unusual ones.

Today it is apparent that many scientists can no longer regard dinosaurs as reptiles, not even very unusual reptiles. The principal reason for this stems from the increasing suspicions that dinosaurs were high users of energy.

Following through on these suspicions, many workers have turned up considerable information that is inconsistent with the assumption that Owen made back in 1841—that dinosaurs were "cold-blooded" (ectothermic).

One of the very first suspicions arises when one compares what is believed to be true about dinosaurs with what is actually known about their nearest living relative, the crocodile.

The crocodile, in scientific terms, includes all crocodiles, alligators, gavials, and caimans. What is unusual about them is that they alone among living reptiles have a four-chamber heart. This would be expected of an endothermic animal— an animal whose blood temperature is maintained by internal controls at a level that is independent of the weather outside the body. And, sure enough, the crocodile has a high level of endothermy—higher than other reptiles, but lower than mammals.

But that is not all. Crocodiles are good parents; they are protective of their eggs, which is a very unreptilelike form of behavior. Finally, it is notable that among reptiles only crocodiles have a voice, which we know at least one group of dinosaurs, the Hadrosaurs, possessed. These and other similarities between the closest related survivor of the ruling reptile group tended to send scholars scurrying and scrounging for more information. It is certainly not enough to make any decisions relative to the dinosaurs, but the uniqueness of the crocodiles stands out when we realize they are the nearest relatives.

One other important observation can be seen when a comparison is made between dinosaurs and the present-day reptiles and amphibians. All living ectothermic animals are sprawlers, but all the endothermic *land* animals have an upright carriage, with the body higher off the ground.

Why then are present-day reptiles sprawlers, while most dinosaurs were not? Could it be because dinosaurs were not reptiles?

Another consideration relates to characteristics exhibited by some newly discovered dinosaurs. For example, it has long been held impossible for dinosaurs to achieve the mammalian level of existence simply because they had small brains. It is true that some dinosaur groups, such as the Stegosaurs and Sauropods, had ridiculously small brains. But consider the newly discovered Predacious dinosaur *Deinonychus* (see Chapter 9).

John Ostrom, who discovered Deinonychus in 1964, adjudged it to have most undinosaurian behavior. It was a swift, sleek-lined, biped that obviously tyrannized the world around it. Its whole appearance denied a low metabolic rate (characteristic of reptiles). Here was a dinosaur—and there is no doubt at all that it is a dinosaur—with a degree of sophistication totally inconsistent with its class. Unfortunately, its brain size is not known. However, it had a one-legged balancing ability, very big eyes, complex phalangeal and limb anatomy, and a specialized, formidable weapon in its five-inch, sickle-shaped claw. This was a specialized dinosaur predator—a refined killing machine.

But while Deinonychus argued against a reptilian classification because of its own set of particular traits and characteristics, there were many other dinosaurs with other kinds of characteristics which also argued against their being members of the reptile class.

One of the chief mysteries in the study of evolution is why the mammals remained in a biological backwater for 140 million years. During all this time, the dinosaurs reigned supreme, occupying all the important large-size and medium-size niches in every land environment.

The mystery stems from the known fact that endothermic animals have a superior advantage over ectothermic animals (reptiles, for example). That advantage is due to the ability to regulate thermal levels within the body by provision of large amounts of energy on short notice (that is, get up a high metabolic rate quickly), or preserve the body's heat system against sudden or prolonged losses of heat through cold or bleak weather conditions. Endothermic animals do this by developing hair, feathers, or thick skin. In addition, endothermic animals have a cell-by-cell heat-producing mechanism that is about four times higher than in reptiles. If necessary, extra heat can be produced by shivering and other physiologic activity.

Thus, endothermic animals would be expected to take over

the environment from reptiles. But they did not. They could not do so until the ruling reptiles died out. Why? Could it be because the ruling reptiles were also endothermic?

That is the conclusion of Robert T. Bakker, one of a vanguard of paleontologists who have recently argued for reclassifying the dinosaurs. The most cogent argument of Bakker and others is a three-pronged assault on the continued practice of classifying dinosaurs as reptiles. This work was aided immensely by the computer-age technology and by other spin-off benefits of science in war and in space exploration.

The first argument derives from studies in bone histology (the study of tissue and structure in bones). These studies were provided mainly by John Ostrom in the United States and Armand Ricqlès in France, beginning in about 1969. Bone is an active tissue that contributes to forming blood cells and helps to maintain a calcium-phosphate balance. The latter is necessary for the proper functioning of other tissues.

In ectotherms, such as the modern reptiles, there is less demand for blood-cell work and calcium-phosphate regulating. Consequently, the bone tissue in ectotherms shows a low-activity pattern—that is, a lower density of blood vessels and fewer *Haversian canals* (the tiny grooves and channels in which vessels sit in a bone). In addition to these differences, the bone histology of endothermic animals shows very little growth ringing. The latter is a strong, seasonal growth in bone layers, seen in ectotherms when they are forced to spend parts of the year hibernating or in dormancy. On both counts, the dinosaur bones appear much more similar to mammals than to reptiles.

The second argument against the dinosaurs as reptiles, proposed by Bakker and colleagues, is the one provided for by the various proofs of Continental Drift. See Chapter 6.

Since paleomagnetism makes possible the reconstruction

of ancient continent positions, the zones of temperature can be plotted for each continent. Such plots have shown that dinosaurs cut across all the zones—they are proven to have existed in cooler climates as well as warmer ones. In contrast, although small modern reptiles such as lizards may live as far north as Canada in North America, the larger reptiles are restricted to warm climates. It would be very surprising indeed for a farmer in Ontario to walk out into his backyard and be forced to chase an alligator away from his chickens. But dinosaurs lived in even cooler climates than those of modern Ontario. That supports the Bakker-Ostrom-Ricqlès conclusion (among others) that dinosaurs were not reptiles. They may very well have had fur, hair, feathers, thick skin, or any combination of these, plus a high endothermy and high metabolic rate. All the facts seem to point in that direction.

Finally, we come to the last argument of major importance. It is an argument based mainly on Bakker's studies regarding the ratio of meat-eating animals (predators) to plant-eating animals (prey).

The ratio of predator to prey is greatly reduced in birds and mammals, due to the high energy needs of these animals. The required amount of meat per predator was higher in dinosaurs than in the more ancient mammallike reptiles and in the earliest reptiles. This indicates a higher metabolic rate, and more active life. The lower the ratio of predator to prey, the higher the heat production per animal. The predator-prey ratios were nearly as low in dinosaurs as in mammals and were far lower than in modern reptiles.

In addition, many authorities now agree that an erect posture—living up on four legs or two legs with the tail as a balancing instrument—is an indication of higher metabolism, higher activity level, and greater heat generating.

Bone histology, predator-prey ratios, climatic zoning, and

the physiology and anatomy of the animals all have been offered as proof that dinosaurs were not reptiles in the modern sense of that term.

THE OPPOSITION. Alan Feduccia of the University of North Carolina opposed the Ostrom-Bakker view as early as 1972. In one paper, Feduccia denied that dinosaurs ever had an activity level equal to that of birds or the large mammals. He claimed that a confusion of terms and nomenclature in the Ostrom-Bakker studies had led to the hasty judgment that dinosaurs were endothermic.

He further pointed out that the dinosaurian joint mechanisms are typical of reptiles and are not nearly as complex as in mammals.

Erect posture, the existence of air spaces in some dinosaur bones, and other features, which are postulated to have contributed to or which may be responsible for endothermy, are, according to Feduccia and others, merely the facets of a complex evolution toward a structural system that would more adequately support heavy weight.

Opponents of the dinosaurs as endothermic animals consistently bring up the problem of brain size. The size of the dinosaur brain would simply exclude the organized physiological levels achieved in mammals.

Another criticism, mainly by Feduccia, but also expressed by others, is that many paleontologists look upon the reptiles and amphibians as primitive lines which serve the endothermic animals as prey, and that the reverse is just not typical.

But it is pointed out that crocodiles, pit vipers, and other modern reptiles do very often feed at the expense of mammals and birds. The prey is often a mammal or bird. This does not lend itself to an argument that ectotherms are born losers in evolution. These same authorities also deny that being "cold-blooded" is an evolutionary disadvantage. They point to the fact that some of the success of modern reptiles is due in fact to their great ability to adjust to seasonal and daily temperature fluctuations by simply lowering their energy levels. Thus, they are most successful in the tropics, where mammals are at a disadvantage.

In one scientific paper, published in 1972 by Albert F. Bennett and Bonnie Dalzell (University of California at Berkeley), the authors delivered a telling blow to Bakker's argument that big dinosaurs were galloping animals, obviously using up a lot of energy running. They pointed out that the mechanisms that permitted galloping in big mammals were inadequately developed in the large dinosaurs. Whatever the outcome, there is little doubt that workers defending the traditional view of dinosaurs as reptiles are on the defensive. They offer many appealing arguments, but unfortunately, most of these are barbs of opposing views directed at other scholars. Little of this opposing view gets into the public media where it can be synthesized to a level at which nonspecialists can comprehend the views.

Actually, there is a consistent communication gap between the paleontologist on the one hand, and the interested amateur, student, general reader, and nonspecialist on the other. This results from a habit of ignoring those who cannot immediately respond or contribute to the dialogues. But the paramount need among scholars today is a double dialogue—one between the scholar and his colleagues, and one directed to young people and the general public, so that they, too, may be stimulated to participate in the heritage of the exciting science of paleontology.

Part of the great success of the proendothermic forces— besides a growing pile of supportive fossil evidence—is based on a discovered evolutionary relationship of dinosaurs to birds. Here too, the traditional view is being altered, and not without opposition. However, the opposing viewpoint does not deny that dinosaurs and birds are closely related—everyone agrees that they are. But many simply deny that this relationship is a linear one—that dinosaurs are not extinct, but still exist—as birds. Let us now consider this relationship between dinosaurs and birds.

CHAPTER 14

Dinosaurs and Birds

Did one species of dinosaur evolve into birds? There were scientists as far back as the 1850s who suspected birds and dinosaurs were related. The evolutionists were sure of it. Charles Darwin's *Origin of Species* was published in 1859. Two years later, a sensational discovery was made in Germany that went a long way toward insuring the success of Darwin's theory of evolution and toward solving the question of bird-dinosaur kinship.

According to Darwin, all life was related. One animal group evolved from another, and by natural selection. The process began with the first single-celled life in the Cryptozoic eon, continues right up to human beings, and is still going on.

Evolutionists spend much of their time comparing the great groups of living things seeking to find which evolved from which. The broad outlines are known.

There is an almost unbroken chain of evolution: fish, to amphibians, to reptiles, to mammals, to humans. Where do the birds and dinosaurs fit? Darwin believed the dinosaurs evolved from primitive reptiles, and the birds evolved from the dinosaurs. But there was a "missing link." If Darwin was right, there should be found somewhere the fossil of an animal that would have the features of both dinosaurs and birds. Antievolutionists were quick to point out how many missing links there appeared to be.

But in 1862, at a quarry in Solnhofen, Bavaria (near Nürnberg, now in West Germany), there turned up a crow-sized skeleton. It had long claws, a tail, and just the hint of teeth.

There was an immediate reaction of joy throughout the scientific world. The creature unearthed appeared to be a reptile, and any scientist in the world would have identified this creature as a dinosaur, except for one single fact: *It had feathers.* Here was a reptile with feathers—the missing link that evolutionists were looking for?

After bitter arguments and a sensational round of dialogues, the scientific world split on the issue. There was doubt. It arose because the animal had a collar bone, and the nearest obvious relative, a small Coelurosaurian dinosaur, had no collar bone. For this reason, paleontologists shied away from stating that the fossil bird was in reality a small dinosaur that was in the stages of becoming a bird.

The fossil was named *Archaeopteryx* (ark-ee-OP-ter-ricks), meaning "ancient wing." The argument on the missing link and the origin of birds was pretty much in abeyance until revived in the 1970s. The whole question was opened up again because of new dinosaur discoveries. Some better Archaeopteryx specimens were found too.

Several paleontologists, taking note of the new attitude toward endothermy in dinosaurs, speculated that Archaeopteryx was really a dinosaur. The proof that it was indeed a dinosaur, and not a bird, appears for the first time to be unequivocal, backed by the discovery of very nearly the same type of skeletons, *with collar bones,* but they were definitely dinosaurs, taken from the rocks of Mongolia. Further studies of Archaeopteryx showed that it had other characteristics not

Archaeopteryx

About the size of a crow

Fig. 30. The first fossils of Archaeopteryx discovered were thought to be those of reptiles—until one was found with traces of feathers on it! Many paleontologists now believe that the bird's nearest dinosaur kin were also feathered. In fact, feathered dinosaurs may have been common. That, of course, would prove that birds are a modern form of the dinosaur biology.

before noticed that were distinctly nonavian, not birdlike. By 1976, Archaeopteryx was known to be a very good missing link. It was believed to have been flightless, it had a tail, it had teeth, and it had several other dinosaur features. Its nearest relative was definitely a small Coelurosaurian dinosaur.

Discoveries made in the Soviet Union within the past few years have given support to the ever-closer link between birds and dinosaurs. One small lizardlike creature named *Longisquama* was a Thecodont covered with long, overlapping scales. These scale structures are almost certainly intermediate forms of feathers.

Further evidence to support a close link between birds and dinosaurs is indirect. It stems from the discovery that some flying reptiles had developed fur or hairlike feathers, which demonstrates conclusively that these reptiles were endothermic. That makes it much easier to believe that one or more early dinosaurian groups were endothermic.

Casting about for likely examples from which the birds may have evolved, we meet up again with our ferocious friend *Deinonychus*—the one with the death-dealing claw. Comparisons between this dinosaur and bird anatomy shows virtually identical details! Except for size. Deinonychus is not the bird's ancestor, because this animal is late in time, but the ancestor is not far removed and is probably also the ancestor of Deinonychus. The big difference between the situation now and bird-dinosaur ideas twenty years ago is that we don't have to go far back into the Triassic period, more than 200 million years ago, to find the immediate ancestor of the bird. It is a dinosaur.

And this is the main reason why many authorities now agree that a new system of classification is called for, one which gives recognition to the fact that at least one, and perhaps more types of *dinosaurs did survive the great crisis at*

the end of the Cretaceous period, and they went on to success-
fully populate the world as birds. To quote a leading paleontologist, Dr. John Ostrom, ". . . the avian radiation is an
aerial exploitation of basic dinosaur physiology and structure. . . ."

In reality, **birds are flying dinosaurs.** As such, the dinosaurs are salvaged from extinction as a class, or as two orders
of endothermic reptiles—we don't yet know how they will be
classified. But there is little doubt that flying dinosaurs are
still in great trouble and are going through another crisis—
this one brought on by the explosive exploitation and over-
population of the earth by their competitive adversaries, a
type of mammal with a big brain—and an even bigger ego to
go with it—human beings.

CHAPTER 15

The Scientific Classification of Dinosaurs

The supportive evidence provided by bone histology, predator-prey relationships, climatic zonation, and other data point to a closer kinship with birds and mammals than with modern reptiles. Two paleontologists, Peter Galton and Robert Bakker, have advocated putting the dinosaurs, birds, and early Thecodont reptiles in a new class known as *Archosauria*. For them, this classification gives support to the idea that dinosaurs are not really extinct—the living birds carry on the basic dinosaur biology.

Another suggested classification is that of A. J. Desmond, who proposes the classes *Dinosauria* (on a level equivalent to that of the reptile class), which would include birds and a number of dinosaurian precursor (ancestral) animals; and *Pterosauria*, the flying reptiles. The two classes would be combined in the superclass *Endosauropsida*. Neither of these classifications have been accepted, and there is not likely to be any action on classification just yet. However, evidence is growing stronger that dinosaurs are ready to move out of the reptile class. As we shall see, they may very well take the birds (class *Aves*) along to wherever they may wind up in the classification tables. It looks as if the dinosaurs are about to be distinguished as a separate class, or superclass to which birds may be added.

INTERNAL CLASSIFICATION. Until a clear agreement can be worked out showing where the dinosaurs fit in the evolutionary column, they cannot be linked *taxonomically* with the rest of the animal kingdom (taxonomy is the science that deals with evolutionary relationships between all animals, and classifies them).

The internal classification—the scientific classification within the two orders of dinosaurs—is given here as an aid to further study. There is no strict agreement in this classification either, but the following one is the most popular and probably is the most acceptable of the several variations that are in existence:

Order Surischia (the lizard-hipped group)
Suborder Theropoda (meat-eating, mostly bipedal)
Infraorder Coelurosauria (the Coelurosaurians), small swift, bipedal carnivorous animals, derived from the Thecodonts.
Families—There are at least six, of which only two have been considered in this book: Coelophysis and Ornithomimus are representative examples.

Infraorder Carnosauria (includes all Theropods that are definitely carnivorous); nearly synonymous with the group in this book known as the Deinodonts. See page 91.
Families—Our only samples are the Tyrannosaurs, of which *Tyrannosaurus rex* is the one genus named in this book, plus Antrodenus and the Gorgosaurs. There are at least four families of Carnosaurs.

Infraorder Prosauropoda (the Prosauropods) the one representative in this book is *Plateosaurus.*
There are three families of Prosauropods.

Suborder Sauropoda (the Sauropods) These are the giant four-footed, plant-eating dinosaurs.

Families—There are two major ones, but the animals shown in this book belong to the Brachiosauridae family, of which *Brachiosaurus* is the prime representative.

Order Ornithischia (the bird-hipped group)

Suborder Ornithopoda This is a very large group. The four main families are represented in this book by one dinosaur each—Hypsilophodon, Iguanodon, a Hadrosaur (*Corythosaurus* is our example), and the dome-headed dinosaurs (our example was *Pachycephalosaurus*).

Suborder Stegosauria (plated dinosaurs)

One family, the Stegosaurs

Suborder Ankylosauria (armored dinosaurs)

There are two families. Our example is a Nodosaur, family Nodosauridae (the Ankylosaur).

Suborder Ceratopsia (horned dinosaurs—Ceratopsians)

There are three major families. Our example is from Ceratopsidae, the large-horn dinosaurs, of which Triceratops is representative.

Note that this or any other classification is always arranged to show which animals evolved first. The list reads from oldest to most recent or last dinosaurs. Thus, the Saurischians are first, and within that order, the meat-eating animals evolved first. The Ceratopsians were the last dinosaurs to evolve and the last to die out.

Epilogue

There is an object lesson in the fall of the dinosaurs. They ruled the earth for a period far longer than the mammals have ruled. Moreover, human beings have been supreme only for a few thousand years—the Age of Human Beings is but a second of time compared to the time the dinosaurs ruled the earth. Yet, the downfall of this highly successful kingdom was a natural event, brought on by a long series of small events. Every volcano that erupted, and every stream of lava that flowed down a hillside in the ancient continent of Pangaea was a nail in the coffin of the dinosaur kingdom. For the cracking apart of Pangaea was the main event, and that started before the dinosaurs even appeared, more than 250 million years ago. Thus it took 180 million years to achieve their destruction.

In the dimension of time, the present is almost as insignificant as the earth is in the universe, where it rates as a mere pinpoint of borrowed light. It is as impossible to comprehend the total span of time during which the dinosaurs lived as it is to comprehend the distance from our solar system to the nearest star. The best we can achieve is to expand our horizons in both time and space in the hopes that doing so will give us the wisdom that will prevent us from joining the dinosaurs in oblivion. Our victory in this respect would be comparable to what one very special dinosaur did when it took on feathers and flew away to join us, as a bird, in our modern world.

GLOSSARY

Albedo (al-BEE-doh)   The ratio of light reflected by the earth to that which it receives from the sun. The albedo of the earth is such that normally about one-third of the light it receives is reflected back into space. Pollutants in the air can change the earth's albedo.

Allosaurus   The former name of Antrodemus.

Anatosaurus   An alternate name for Trachodon, a classic duck-billed dinosaur.

Ankylosaurus (AN-kee-loh-sawr-us)   The principal Cretaceous armored dinosaur.

Antrodemus (an-TROH-dee-mus)   Massive Jurassic Theropod predator.

Apatosaurus (a-PAT-oh-sawr-us)   A big Jurassic Sauropod dinosaur; also known as Brontosaurus, an older, perhaps obsolete name.

Archaeopteryx (ar-kee-OP-ter-icks)   The earliest discovered bird; of Jurassic age.

Armored Dinosaur   *See* Ankylosaurus.

Brachiosaurus (brack-ee-oh-SAWR-us)   The largest of all Sauropod dinosaurs; weighed up to sixty tons; the Brachiosauridae is the principal family of Sauropod dinosaurs.

Brontosaurus   *See* Apatosaurus.

Cacops (KA-kops)   A Permian period amphibian.

Cambrian Period   The first period of the Paleozoic era; began 600 million years ago and lasted 80 million years.

Camptosaurus   An early Ornithischian dinosaur; the primary ancestral form of the Hadrosaurs.

Carboniferous Period   Fifth period of the Paleozoic era; it is the European designation for the two American periods, Mississippian and Pennsylvanian; Carboniferous began 385 million years ago and lasted 70 million years.

Catastrophism   A doctrine in early modern science which supported the Christian scriptural interpretation that a Great Deluge had occurred a few thousand years ago. Some of its adherents also backed a multiple-deluge theory.

Cenozoic Era   The present era; also known as the Age of Mammals; it began 70 million years ago, when the dinosaurs died out.

Ceratopsia   The suborder of Ornithischian horned dinosaurs.

Ceratosaurus (seh-RAT-oh-sawr-us)   The only horned carnivorous dinosaur known; may be a special variant of Antrodemus.

Coelophysis (see-loh-FAHY-sis)   Small, ferocious, bipedal ancestor of the giant Theropod dinosaurs of later times.

Coelurosaurus (SEE-loo-roh-sawr-us)   The infraorder of small bipeds to which coelophysis belonged.

Compsognathus (comp-sog-NATH-us)   The smallest known dinosaur; its anatomy is remarkably similar to that of the early birds.

Continental Drift   The theory originated by Alfred Wegener, now generally accepted as a means of explaining the present world land positions, gross features, and worldwide geologic events.

Corythosaurus (koh-ree-thoh-SAWR-us)   One of several types of hollow-crested Hadrosaurs.

Cotylosaurus (KOT-ee-loh-sawr-us)   The first true reptiles; known as stem reptiles, they gave rise to birds, flying reptiles, crocodiles, and dinosaurs.

Cretaceous Period   The last period of the Mesozoic era; began 145 million years ago and lasted 70 million years. It is the time during which the dinosaurs reached their highest stage of development; the period ended with the extinction of all dinosaurs.

Cryptozoic (KRIP-toh-zoh-ick) **eon**   All the vast span of time in the earth's history before animals and plants appeared as fossils in the rocks.

Deinodont (DEH-noh-dont)   The "terrible tooth" dinosaurs; they were the large predators of the Jurassic and Cretaceous periods.

Deinonychus (deh-non-EE-kus)   A small, swift, fierce predator; one of the Dromeosaurs; may have been on a direct line of evolution toward birds, and it may have been a warm-blooded animal (endotherm).

Devonian Period   Fourth period of the Paleozoic era; began 440 million years ago and lasted 55 million years. It is known as the Age of Fishes.

Dimetrodon (dahy-MEE-troh-don)   A Pelycosaur; representative of one of the reptiles that gave rise to mammal-like reptiles and mammals.

Diplodocus (dahy-PLOH-doh-kus)   The longest of all dinosaurs; a contemporary of the Jurassic Apatosaurus; it represents the popular idea of a dinosaur.

Duck-billed Dinosaurs   The very large group of dinosaurs that are known to paleontologists as Hadrosaurs; many had strange head shapes and various crests; all were bipedal, probably aquatic some of the time, and highly sensitive to sound and sight.

Ectothermic   The proper term to use instead of "cold-bloodedness"; means that an animal's blood temperature fluctuates within a narrow range under the influence of weather temperatures for at least part of its life; a less-used but also accurate term is *poikilothermic*.

Endothermic   The proper term to be used instead of "hot-blooded" or "warm-blooded"; means that an animal has at least some internal blood temperature-regulating mechanism that can help maintain a steady blood temperature despite most normal weather conditions. A less-used but accurate alternate term with the same meaning is *homoiothermic*.

Euparkeria   An early Thecodont reptile; regarded as the immediate ancestor of all dinosaurs; it is of early Triassic age.

Eurypterids (you-RIP-ter-ids)   A group of Ordovician age animals that resembled the modern scorpions and which were related to them, and to crabs, crayfish, spiders, lobsters, etc. Some of them grew to six feet or more in length. They were the largest animals of their time.

Evolution   A body of knowledge based on the theory that all organisms have developed from simpler ancestors over long periods of time by means of natural selection. The theory of evolution answers so many questions of animal origin and relationship that it enjoys almost universal support in science.

Extinction   The dying out of all members of one type of animal or plant. Some examples: the dying out of all cats or all dogs or all dinosaurs.

Fossils   The hard parts of plants and animals, or a record of life, such as footprints, preserved in the rocks by natural processes for long periods of time.

Geochronology   The science of determining the age of the earth's major features, landforms, and rock layers.

Geomagnetism   The science of earth magnetism and the earth's magnetic force field.

Global Geology   The new science discipline that deals with worldwide natural phenomena and seeks to trace all the consequences or results of such phenomena for the future and the past history of the earth.

Gondwanaland   The postulated southern supercontinent thought to have comprised what is now Africa, South America, Antarctica, Australia, plus Madagascar, the subcontinent of India, and perhaps other parts of southern and eastern Asia. It began to break up about 260 million years ago.

Gorgosaurus   One of the Cretaceous period Deinodonts; it is thought by some to have been a scavenger rather than a predator.

Hadrosaur   The scientific designation for all the duck-billed dinosaurs of the suborder Ornithopoda.

Haversian Canals   Grooves or channels in bone tissue where blood vessels are embedded or attached. The study of these structures reveals information on endothermy and ectothermy.

Homoiothermic   *See* Endothermic.

Horned Dinosaurs   The Ceratopsian suborder which includes Triceratops and all its immediate ancestral forms.

Hypsilophodon (hip-sih-LOH-foh-don)   A Cretaceous Ornithischian dinosaur that retains traits of its primitive ancestors; it has been used to try and reconstruct a model of the earliest Ornithischians, which have not been found as fossils yet.

Ichthyosauria (ick-thee-oh-SAWR-ee-uh)   A giant marine reptile, unrelated to the dinosaurs, although it was a contemporary.

Ichthyostega (ick-thee-oh-STAY-guh)   The first four-footed animal; an early Labyrinthodont amphibian—the ancestor of all land animals.

Iguanodon   A large, bipedal, Ornithischian dinosaur; the first to be discovered as fossils.

Jurassic Period   The second period of the Mesozoic era; began 210 million years ago and lasted 65 million years; it is the central of the three periods of the Age of Dinosaurs.

Laurasia   The postulated northern supercontinent; believed to have included North America, Greenland, Europe, and western Asia. Before it broke up, beginning about 260 million years ago, it may have been part of Pangaea, the supercontinent that included all the present continents.

Limnocelis   An early Cotylosaur or stem reptile.

Mantle   The layer of the earth beginning just under the crust and extending downward for 1,800 miles; it is the main source of heat and rock material moved about in plate tectonics.

Megalosaurus   A European Theropod dinosaur; one of those studied by Sir Richard Owen before deciding to establish the dinosaurs as a group separate from the prehistoric lizards.

Mesozoic Era   Comprises the three periods of the Age of Dinosaurs; began 260 million years ago and lasted 190 million years, ending 70 million years ago when the dinosaurs died out.

Mississippian Period The fifth period of the Paleozoic era; began 385 million years ago and lasted 40 million years; in Europe it is regarded as the lower part of the Carboniferous period; it is known as the Age of Coal.

Monoclonius One of the largest horned dinosaurs.

Mosasaurus (moh-suh-SAWR-us) A giant marine lizard; the first prehistoric reptile to be carefully studied; it was classified as a reptile by Baron Cuvier, whose decision to call it a reptile influenced all the subsequent studies of prehistoric animals.

Natural Selection The evolutionary process that depends upon the chance appearance of useful mutations in order to advance the higher probabilities that an organism will survive long enough to reproduce. Chance useful mutations are the means by which plants and animals evolve.

Nodosaurus The group of armored dinosaurs to which belongs the principal animal, Ankylosaur.

Ordovician Period Second period of the Paleozoic era; began 520 million years ago and lasted 55 million years. It is the central period of the Age of Marine Invertebrates.

Ornithischia (or-nee-THIS-kee-uh) The second of two orders of dinosaurs; they were the bird-hipped dinosaurs.

Ornithomimus An early bipedal Theropod dinosaur; it looked a little like an ostrich and is called the ostrich dinosaur, though it bears no relationship to an ostrich.

Ornithopoda A suborder of Ornithischians that includes four main families, but principally the duck-billed dinosaurs.

Oviraptor (oh-vee-RAP-tor) The name given to some Ornithomimid dinosaurs because it is believed that they robbed eggs from other dinosaurs.

Pachycephalosaurus (pack-ee-SEF-uh-loh-sawr-us)   The bone-head dinosaurs; they are somewhat related to the Hadrosaurs (duck-billed dinosaurs).

Paleogeomagnetism   Earth magnetism in the distant geologic past. A record of changes in the earth's force field is contained in many rocks, and some of this record furnishes proof of Continental Drift and other phenomena.

Paleontology   The study of life in the distant past.

Paleozoic Era   The first era of the Phanerozoic eon; it began 600 million years ago and lasted 340 million years; it is divided into seven periods—six in Europe—and includes the Age of Invertebrates, Age of Fishes, Age of Amphibians, and part of the Age of Reptiles.

Pangaea (pan-GEE-uh)   The postulated ancient supercontinent that is believed to have existed near the end of the Paleozoic era and which may have split into two continents (Laurasia and Gondwanaland) before disintegrating completely to form the present continents.

Pelycosaur   *See* Dimetrodon.

Pennsylvanian Period   Sixth period of the Paleozoic era; began 345 million years ago and lasted 30 million years. In Europe it is regarded as the upper portion of the Carboniferous period—the Age of Coal. It is also sometimes referred to as the Age of Cockroaches (there were six-inch roaches in Pennsylvanian period forests) and as the Age of Amphibians.

Permian Period   Seventh and last period of the Paleozoic era; began 315 million years ago and lasted 55 million years. It began the Age of Reptiles, but ended in a great crisis for all living things, which ended the era.

Phanerozoic Eon   The span of time during which life has been known and visible through the existence of fossils; it began 600 million years ago and is still in progress.

Phytosaur (FAHY-toh-sawr)   Strange crocodilelike reptiles, unrelated to crocodiles or dinosaurs; they are an example of evolutionary convergence, the evolving of similar shapes in unrelated animals (Ichthyosaurs and modern dolphins are another example).

Plankton   The mass of floating tiny creatures and plants that form the basis of the world's marine food chain, now as well as throughout the past. Plankton is divided into *Phytoplankton*, the plants, and *Zooplankton*, the animals.

Plated Dinosaurs   The Stegosaurs.

Plateosaurus   A Prosauropod dinosaur; the ancestor of large Jurassic age Sauropods such as Diplodocus and Apatosaurus.

Plate Tectonics   The complex science of moving crustal plates; it involves the use of geophysical, seismological, and other types of data for the purpose of determining, measuring, predicting, and recording the history of crustal plate movements. It is founded on the theory of Continental Drift, and the theory of seafloor spreading.

Plesiosaur (PLEE-see-oh-sawr)   A Jurassic-Cretaceous marine reptile; unrelated to dinosaurs. Sensational reports of its continued existence in the Pacific Ocean have been issued, but as of late 1977, no reliable scientific evidence was yet available. Should it prove to be a true report, the effects on dinosaur studies would be revolutionary, since the animal was a contemporary of dinosaurs. Most scientists are highly skeptical.

Polacanthus   One of the armored dinosaurs, although it greatly resembles the plated dinosaurs (Stegosaurs).

Prosauropod   *See* Plateosaurus.

Pseudomorph (soo-doh-morf)   The name used to describe fossils discovered by the early Christians. Fossils were thought to be forms and shapes which God experimented with and rejected. He left the rejects in the rocks as fossils.

Psittacosaurus (SIT-uh-ko-sawr-us)   An early Ceratopsian or horned dinosaur; quite possibly the ancestor of all horned dinosaurs.

Pterosaur (TER-oh-sawr)   An extinct order of flying reptiles; unrelated to the dinosaurs or birds, but they did evolve from the same Thecodont ancestors as the dinosaurs.

Saurischia (sawr-ISK-ee-uh)   The first of two orders of dinosaurs—the lizard-hipped group, to which belong nearly all the carnivorous dinosaurs, and the large, Sauropod herbivorous dinosaurs.

Sauropoda   The suborder of Saurischians to which the large, grazing Sauropods belong.

Silurian Period   The third period of the Paleozoic era; began 465 million years ago and lasted 25 million years. It is the shortest of all the periods. Plants began to invade the land and insects appeared.

Stromatolites (stroh-MAT-oh-lahyt)   A Calcareous structure made up of the remains of tiny blue-green algae plants. Stromatolites of blue-green algae have been found that are 2.3 billion years old. These algae are the very first forms of life to be recorded in the rocks, and thus are the oldest organisms known.

Styracosaurus (STAHY-ruh-ko-sawr-us)   An early Ceratopsian or horned dinosaur.

Subduction   The geophysical and geological process that acts very slowly to destroy the ocean floor by drawing or plunging it downward into the mantle where it is melted. This occurs at deep-sea trenches as a result of lateral pressures generated by crustal plate movement. Subduction is basic to plate tectonics and the theory of Continental Drift.

Superposition   The geological principal that layers of rocks above are younger than layers below in a particular undisturbed formation of rocks. This principal is used as an aid in age determination in geology.

Thecodont (THEE-koh-dont) The small, bipedal ancestor of all dinosaurs. See Euparkeria.

Theropoda A suborder of Saurischian carnivorous dinosaurs; it includes all the largest predators, and a good many of the smaller types, too.

Trachodon The largest of all the duck-billed dinosaurs.

Triassic Period The first period of the Mesozoic era; began 260 million years ago and lasted 50 million years. It is the first of the three periods in the Age of Dinosaurs, although these animals did not evolve until late in the period.

Triceratops The greatest of all the Ceratopsian, or horned, dinosaurs, and the last dinosaur to die out.

Trilobite (TRAHY-loh-bahyt) The early Paleozoic ruler of the earth, although it never exceeded more than a foot or two in diameter. It was an invertebrate, but was the most advanced animal of the Cambrian period, the first period of the Paleozoic era.

Tyrannosaurus Rex A genus of Theropod Deinodont, or "terrible tooth," dinosaurs. It is regarded as the most powerful animal that ever lived, and probably one of the fiercest.

Uniformitarianism Also known as actualism; the doctrine that all the agents of geologic change, such as weathering, volcanism, and diastrophism (mountain building) that have occurred in the past have operated over long periods of time in exactly the same manner as they operate today. Thus, erosion and weathering are the same processes that went on in the past and were just as effective then as they are today.

BIBLIOGRAPHY

Bakker, Robert T. "Dinosaur Renaissance." *Scientific American,* April 1975, pp. 58–79.

———. "Dinosaur Physiology and the Origin of Mammals." *Evolution,* no. 25 (1968), pp. 636–658.

Calder, Nigel. *The Restless Earth: A Report on the New Geology.* New York: Viking Press, 1972.

Colbert, Edwin H. *Dinosaurs: Their Discovery and Their World.* New York: E. P. Dutton, 1961.

———. *Evolution of the Vertebrates.* New York: E. P. Dutton, 1969.

———. *Wandering Lands and Animals.* New York: E. P. Dutton, 1973.

———. *Men and Dinosaurs.* New York: E. P. Dutton, 1968.

Cowen, Richard. *History of Life.* New York: McGraw-Hill Book Co., 1976.

Cox, Barry. *Prehistoric Animals.* New York: Grosset & Dunlap, 1970.

Desmond, Adrian J. *The Hot-Blooded Dinosaurs.* New York: The Dial Press, 1976.

Dunbar, Carl O. *Historical Geology.* New York: John Wiley & Sons, Inc., 1969.

Eiseley, Loren. *Darwin's Century: Evolution and the Men Who Discovered It.* New York: Anchor Books, 1961.

Kurtén. Björn. *The Age of Dinosaurs.* New York: McGraw-Hill Book Co., 1968.

Mayr, Ernst. *Evolution and the Diversity of Life.* Cambridge, Mass.: Harvard University Press, Belknap Press, 1976.

Ratkevich, Ronald P. *Dinosaurs of the Southwest.* Albuquerque: University of New Mexico Press, 1966.

Scientific American (Readings From). *Continents Adrift.* San Francisco: W. H. Freeman & Co., 1972.

―――. *Planet Earth.* San Francisco: W. H. Freeman & Co., 1974.

Sullivan, Walter. *Continents in Motion.* New York: McGraw-Hill Book Co., 1974.

Zappler, Lisbeth, and Zappler, Georg. *The World after the Dinosaurs.* New York: American Museum of Natural History, 1970.

INDEX

Pacific plate, 59
Paleogeomagnetism, 67–69, 150
Paleontology and paleontologists, 14, 15–16, 22; founding of, 27–37; origin of name, 28; paleontology and catastrophism, 29; growth of paleontology in America, 38, 39, 40; English paleontologists, 32, 150; French, 41, 103
Paleozoic Era, 48, 56, 57, 73, 150
Pangaea, 65, 66, 118–119, 150. *See also* supercontinent
Parasaurolophus, 105
Pelycosaur, 74, 85
Pennsylvanian Period, 52, 150
Permian Period, 54, 72, 150
Peru Trench, 61, 69
Phanerozoic Eon, 48, 150
Photography, in use with fossil hunting, 38
Phytosaur, 85, 150
Planetary geology, 16. *See also* new global geology
Plankton, 50, 151
Plants, earliest, 46, 53; and extinction of dinosaurs, 114, 117
Plated dinosaurs, 105–107, 139, 151
Plateosaurus, 87, 151
Plate tectonics, 16–17, 58, 117
Plesiosaur, 119, 151
Polacanthus, 108, 151
Pope Gregory IX, 20
Predator, 84; predator-prey relationship, 85, 86, 127
"Present is the key to the past," 26
Prosauropoda, 87
Protoceratops, 109
Pseudomorphs, 23, 151
Psittacosaurus, 108–109, 151
Pterosaur, 75, 119; pterosauria, in classification, 137; 152
Puff the Magic Dragon, 12

Ray, John, 26
Religion and science, 22–23, 24
Renaissance, 20–24
Reptile, 14, 28, 30, 33, 34; Age of Reptiles, 56, 71–76; definition of reptile, 77; 114; were dinosaurs reptiles?, 123–130; in classification of dinosaurs, 137–138
Ricqlès, Armand, 126, 127
Romans, 20

San Andreas Fault, 59

San Francisco, 59
Saurischians, 78, 83–97, 139, 152
Saurolophus, 104
Sauropoda, 87–94, 152
Science fiction and dinosaurs, 12
Scientific thought, freedom of, 23, 24
Scopes Trial, 28
Seafloor spreading, theory of, 58, 61
Seely, Harry Govier, 32
Seismology, 56
Silurian Period, 50–51, 152
Smallest dinosaur. *See* Compsognathus
Smith, William, 26, 32
Snake, 14, 74, 114
Soviet Union, recent discoveries in, 134
Special Creation. *See* Creation
Spontaneous generation, 19
Stegosaurus, 105–106, 107
Stem reptile. *See* Cotylosaurus
Steno, Nicolaus, 25
Stratigraphy, 28
Stromatolites, 46, 152
Subduction of plates, 69, 152
Supercontinent, 16, 65
Superposition, 152

Tethys Sea, 65
Tharp, Marie, 57
Thecodont, 74, 75, 82, 83, 84, 99, 153; thecodonts and birds, 134–135
Theropoda, 91–97, 115, 139, 153
Trachodon, 104, 105, 153
Triassic Period, 71, 73, 74, 84, 86, 153
Trilobite, 48, 153
Triceratops, 109, 111, 153
Turtle, 14, 74, 85, 114
Tweed, Boss William, 39
Tyrannosaurus rex, 92–93, 107, 108, 109, 115, 153

Uniformitarianism, 26, 153
Ussher, Archbishop, 21, 22

Volcanism, 120, 141

Warm-blooded, hot-blooded. *See* endothermic
Warm-blooded, cold-blooded argument, 127–129
Wegener, Alfred, 58, 59
Wistar, Caspar, 37

About the Author

William Jaber was born in West Virginia, but spent his childhood in the Midwest. His family returned to West Virginia in 1935, taking up life in a coal-mining community.

Mr. Jaber quit school in 1940 to join the U.S. Army and spent the next five years as a tankman and radio operator.

After World War II, Mr. Jaber elected not to return to his native state, and instead, went to New York City where he resumed his education. He graduated in 1952 from New York University.

He was married in 1947. He and his wife Dorothy raised three children and have one grandchild.

Mr. Jaber's early career was that of a cartographer. He joined the Macmillan firm as staff cartographer in 1961. And it was at Macmillan that Mr. Jaber also began a career in editing and writing. Since that time he has contributed thousands of articles and hundreds of maps and illustrations to reference works and trade books.

In 1967, Mr. Jaber undertook to manage a huge, six-year encyclopedia project, resulting in the publication of *Cadillac Modern Encyclopedia* (1973). Following the completion of this book, Bill adapted himself to a fully free-lance career.